M000201553

A JOURNEY OF RICHES

Motivate Your Life

11 Inspiring stories to move you into action

A Journey Of Riches – Motivate Your Life
11 Inspiring stories to move you into action
Copyright © 2022 John Spender

This work is copyright. Apart from any use as permitted under the Copyright Act 1968, no part may be reproduced, copied, scanned, stored in a retrieval system, recorded, or transmitted, in any form or by any means, without the prior permission of the publisher.

The rights of John Spender to be identified as the primary author of this work have been asserted by him under the Copyright Amendment (Moral Rights) Act 2000 Disclaimer.

The author and publishers have used their best efforts in preparing this book and disclaim liability arising directly and indirectly, consequential, or otherwise, from its contents.

All reasonable efforts have been made to obtain necessary copyright permissions. Any omissions or errors are unintentional and if brought to the attention of the publishers, will be corrected in future impressions and printings.

Published by Motion Media International
Editors: Kit Brookman, Tiffany Oharo, Calvary Diggs, Daniel Decillis, Eric Wyman, and Katie Beck.
Cover Design: Motion Media International
Typesetting & Assembly: Motion Media International
Printing: Amazon and Ingram Sparks

Creator: John Spender - Primary Author
Title: *A Journey of Riches - Motivate Your Life*
ISBN Digital: 978-1-925919-45-5
ISBN Print: 978-1-925919-46-2
Subjects: Motivation, Inspiration

ACKNOWLEDGMENTS

Reading and writing are gifts that very few give to themselves. It is such a powerful way to reflect and gain closure from the past; reading and writing are therapeutic processes. The experience raises one's self-esteem, confidence, and awareness of self.

I learned this when I collated the first book in the *A Journey of Riches* series, which now includes twenty-nine books with over 300 co-authors from over forty different countries. It's difficult to write about your personal experiences, and I honor and respect every author who has collaborated in the series.

For many authors, English is their second language, which is a significant achievement. In creating this anthology of short stories, I have been touched by the generosity, gratitude, and shared energy this experience has given everyone.

The inspiration for A Journey of Riches, Motivate Your Life was born from my desire to write about motivation and the role it can play in your life. Each chapter is written by a different author sharing their depth of wisdom.

I want to thank all the authors for entrusting me with their unique memories, encounters, and wisdom. Thank you for sharing and opening the door to your soul so others may learn from your experience. I trust the readers will gain confidence from your successes, and wisdom, from your failures.

I also want to thank my family. I know you are proud of me, seeing how far I have come from that ten-year-old boy learning how to read and write at a basic level. Big shout out to my Mom, Robert, Dad, Merril; my brother Adam and his daughter Krystal; my sister Hollie, her partner Brian, my nephew Charlie and niece, Heidi;

thank you for your support. Also, kudos to my grandparents, Gran, and Pop, who are alive and well, and Ma and Pa, who now rest in peace. They accept me just the way I am with all my travels and adventures around the world.

Thanks to all the team at Motion Media International; you have done an excellent job at editing and collating this book. It was a pleasure working with you on this successful project, and I thank you for your patience in dealing with the changes and adjustments along the way.

Thank you, the reader, for having the courage to look at your life and how you can improve your future in a fast and rapidly changing world.

Thank you again to my fellow co-authors: Elizabeth Sim, Anthony Dierickx, Kaye Doran, Dario Cucci, Jamie Fair, Hassan Magdy Saad, Belen Lowery, Marcia Quinton, Marie Chandler, and Kelly Wahl.

With gratitude,
John Spender

Praise For *A Journey of Riches* Book Series

"The *A Journey of Riches* book series is a great collection of inspiring short stories that will leave you wanting more!"
~ Alex Hoffmann, Network Marketing Guru.

"If you are looking for an inspiring read to get you through any change, this is it! This book is comprised of many gripping perspectives from a collection of successful international authors with a tone of wisdom to share."
~ Theera Phetmalaigul, Entrepreneur/Investor.

"*A Journey of Riches* is an empowering series that implements two simple words in overcoming life's struggles.

By diving into the meaning of the words "problem" and "challenge," you will find yourself motivated to believe in the triumph of perseverance. With many different authors from all around the world coming together to share various stories of life's trials, you will find yourself drenched in encouragement to push through even the darkest of battles. The stories are heartfelt personal shares of moving through and transforming challenges into rich life experiences.

The book will move, touch, and inspire your spirit to face and overcome any of life's adversities. It is a truly inspirational read. Thank you for being the kind, open soul you are, John!"
~ Casey Plouffe, Seven Figure Network Marketer.

"A must-read for anyone facing major changes or challenges in life right now. This book will give you the courage to move through any struggle with confidence, grace, and ease."
~ Jo-Anne Irwin, Transformational Coach and Best Selling Author.

"I have enjoyed the *Journey of Riches* book series. Each person's story is written from the heart, and everyone's journey is different. We all have a story to tell, and John Spender does an amazing job of finding authors and combining their stories into uplifting books."
~ Liz Misner Palmer, Foreign Service Officer.

"A timely read as I'm facing a few challenges right now. I like the various insights from the different authors. This book will inspire you to move through any challenge or change that you are experiencing."
~ David Ostrand, Business Owner.

"I've known John Spender for a while now, and I was blessed with an opportunity to be in book four in the series. I know that you will enjoy this new journey, like the rest of the books in the series. The collection of stories will assist you with making changes, dealing with challenges, and seeing that transformation is possible for your life."
~ Charlie O' Shea, Entrepreneur.

"*A Journey of Riches* series will draw you in and help you dig deep into your soul. These authors have unbelievable life stories of purpose inside of them. John Spender is dedicated to bringing peace, love, and adventure to the world of his readers! Dive into this series, and you will be transformed!"
~ Jeana Matichak, Author of *Finding Peace*.

"Awesome! Truly inspirational! It is amazing what the human spirit can achieve and overcome! Highly recommended!"
~ FabriceBeliard, Australian Business Coach and Best Selling Author.

"*A Journey of Riches* Series is a must-read. It is an empowering collection of inspirational and moving stories, full of courage, strength, and heart. Bringing peace and awareness to those lucky

enough to read to assist and inspire them on their life journey."
~ Gemma Castiglia, Avalon Healing, Best Selling Author.

"The *A Journey of Riches* book series is an inspirational collection of books that will empower you to take on any challenge or change in life."
~ Kay Newton, Midlife Stress Buster, and Best Selling Author.

"*A Journey of Riches* book series is an inspiring collection of stories, sharing many different ideas and perspectives on how to overcome challenges, deal with change and make empowering choices in your life. Open the book anywhere and let your mood choose where you need to read. Buy one of the books today; you'll be glad that you did!"
~ Trish Rock, Modern Day Intuitive, Best Selling Author, Speaker, Psychic & Holistic Coach.

"*A Journey of Riches* is another inspiring read. The authors are from all over the world, and each has a unique perspective to share that will have you thinking differently about your current circumstances in life. An insightful read!"
~ Alexandria Calamel, Success Coach and Best Selling Author.

"The *A Jour¹ney of Riches* book series is a collection of real-life stories, which are truly inspiring and give you the confidence that no matter what you are dealing with in your life, there is a light at the end of the tunnel, and a very bright one at that. Totally empowering!"
~ John Abbott, Freedom Entrepreneur.

"An amazing collection of true stories from individuals who have overcome great changes, and who have transformed their lives and used their experience to uplift, inspire and support others."
~ Carol Williams, Author, Speaker & Coach.

"You can empower yourself from the power within this book that can help awaken the sleeping giant within you. John has a

purpose in life to bring inspiring people together to share their wisdom for the benefit of all who venture deep into this book series. If you are looking for inspiration to be someone special, this book can be your guide."
~ Bill Bilwani, Renowned Melbourne Restaurateur.

"In the *A Journey of Riches* series, you will catch the impulse to step up, reconsider and settle for only the very best for yourself and those around you. Penned from the heart and with an unflinching drive to make a difference for the good of all, *A Journey of Riches* series is a must-read."
~ Steve Coleman, author of *Decisions, Decisions! How to Make the Right One Every Time.*

"Do you want to be on top of your game? *A Journey of Riches* is a must-read with breakthrough insights that will help you do just that!"
~ Christopher Chen, Entrepreneur.

"In *A Journey of Riches*, you will find the insight, resources, and tools you need to transform your life. By reading the author's stories, you, too, can be inspired to achieve your greatest accomplishments and what is truly possible for you. Reading this book activates your true potential for transforming your life way beyond what you think is possible. Read it and learn how you, too, can have a magical life."
~ Elaine Mc Guinness, Best Selling Author of *Unleash Your Authentic Self!*

"If you are looking for an inspiring read, look no further than the *A Journey of Riches* book series. The books are an inspiring collection of short stories that will encourage you to embrace life even more. I highly recommend you read one of the books today!"
~ Kara Dono, Doula, Healer, and Best Selling Author.

"*A Journey of Riches* series is a must-read for anyone seeking to enrich their own lives and gain wisdom through the wonderful stories of personal empowerment & triumphs over life's challenges. I've given several copies to my family, friends, and clients to inspire

and support them to step into their greatness. I highly recommend that you read these books, savoring the many 'aha's' and tools you will discover inside."
~ Michele Cempaka, Hypnotherapist, Shaman, Transformational Coach & Reiki Master.

"If you are looking for an inspirational read, look no further than the *A Journey of Riches* book series. The books are an inspiring and educational collection of short stories from the author's soul that will encourage you to embrace life even more. I've even given them to my clients, too, so that their journeys inspire them in life for wealth, health, and everything else in between. I recommend you make it a priority to read one of the books today!"
~ Goro Gupta, Chief Education Officer, Mortgage Terminator, Property Mentor.

"The *A Journey of Riches* book series is filled with real-life short stories of heartfelt tribulations turned into uplifting, self-transformation by the power of the human spirit to overcome adversity. The journeys captured in these books will encourage you to embrace life in a whole new way. I highly recommend reading this inspiring anthology series."
~ Chris Drabenstott, Best Selling Author, and Editor.

"There is so much motivational power in the *A Journey of Riches* series!! Each book is a compilation of inspiring, real-life stories by several different authors, which makes the journey feel more relatable and success more attainable. If you are looking for something to move you forward, you'll find it in one (or all) of these books."
~ Cary MacArthur, Personal Empowerment Coach.

"I've been fortunate to write with John Spender, and now, I call him a friend. *A Journey of Riches* book series features real stories that have inspired me and will inspire you. John has a passion for finding amazing people from all over the world, giving the series a global perspective on relevant subject matters."
~ Mike Campbell, Fat Guy Diary, LLC.

"The *A Journey of Riches* series is the reflection of beautiful souls who have discovered the fire within. Each story takes you inside the truth of what truly matters in life. While reading these stories, my heart space expanded to understand that our most significant contribution in this lifetime is to give and receive love. May you also feel inspired as you read this book."
~ Katie Neubaum, Author of *Transformation Calling*.

"*A Journey of Riches* is an inspiring testament that love and gratitude are the secret ingredients to living a happy and fulfilling life. This series is sure to inspire and bless your life in a big way. Truly an inspirational read that is written and created by real people, sharing real-life stories about the power and courage of the human spirit."
~ Jen Valadez, Emotional Intuitive and Best Selling Author.

TABLE OF CONTENTS

PREFACE

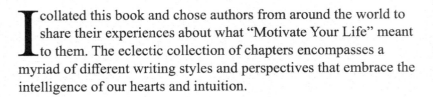

I collated this book and chose authors from around the world to share their experiences about what "Motivate Your Life" meant to them. The eclectic collection of chapters encompasses a myriad of different writing styles and perspectives that embrace the intelligence of our hearts and intuition.

Like us all, each author has a unique story and insight to share with you. It might so happen that one or more authors have lived through an experience like one in your life. Their words could be just the words you need to read to help you through your challenges and motivate you to continue your chosen path.

Storytelling has been the way humankind has communicated ideas and learning throughout our civilization. While we have become more sophisticated with technology and living in the modern world is more convenient, there is still much discontent and dissatisfaction. Many people have also moved away from reading books, and they are missing valuable information that can help them move forward in life with a positive outlook. Moving toward the tasks or dreams that scare us breeds confidence in growing towards becoming better versions of ourselves.

I think it is essential to turn off the television, slow down, read, reflect, and take the time to appreciate everything you have in life. Start with an anthology book as they offer a cornucopia of viewpoints relating to a particular theme. Here, it's fear and how others have dealt with it. I think we feel stuck in life or having challenges in a particular area because we see the problem through the same lens that created it. With this compendium and all the books in the *A Journey of Riches* series, you have many writing styles and perspectives that will help you think and see your challenges differently, motivating you to elevate your set of circumstances.

Anthology books are also great because you can start from any chapter and gain valuable insight or a nugget of wisdom without the feeling you have missed something from the earlier episodes.

I love reading many types of personal development books because learning and personal growth are vital. If you are not learning and growing, well, you're staying the same. Everything in the universe is growing, expanding, and changing. If we are not open to different ideas and a multitude of ways to think and be, then even the most skilled and educated among us can become close-minded.

The concept of this book series is to open you up to diverse ways of perceiving your reality. It is to encourage you and give you many avenues of thinking about the same subject. My wish for you is to feel empowered to make a decision that will best suit you in moving forward with your life. As Albert Einstein said, **"We cannot solve problems with the same level of thinking that created them."** With Einstein's words in mind, let your mood pick a chapter, or read from the beginning to the end and be guided to find the answers you seek.

If you feel inspired, we would love an honest review on Amazon. This will help create awareness around this fantastic series of books.

With gratitude,

John Spender

"The only impossible journey is the one you never begin."

~ Tony Robbins

CHAPTER ONE

———∽◦∈∕∕⊃◦∈———

Your Inner Voice of Knowing, Power, and Potential

By Kaye Doran

When John Spender presented me with the opportunity to contribute to this book, I replied with a response that included all the reasons I had previously said no to other offers. I had believed that I would write my book again. A few days later, he replied, addressing each point. He showed me how this opportunity was different, and his message was even woven with a touch of humor – a very different approach from what I usually see.

I realized that I needed to be open to opportunities, rather than closed, and explore my options more thoroughly. I felt motivated and knowing, building within myself as I did this. This feeling of certainty was solidified after a follow-up conversation with John. So now, here I am, writing my chapter… which I never imagined doing!

As always, a little fear stirred within me. Fear will always show itself when a decision is made to move past one's current comfort zone. This was exciting. I had to stretch, trust, and grow. I attached no meaning to why I needed to write in this book. I simply "knew" I had to say yes. My thoughts and my opportunities were in alignment.

The next thing I needed to explore was asking the question, "What does 'motivate your life' mean and what has motivated my life?"

I recall speaking aloud after my prayers with my mother from a very young age. No, we were not deeply religious; however, in my early years, we did regularly attend Sunday school and service, and I was always a very questioning and inquisitive child regarding God, life and the Universe. I would lie in bed and question, "God, I know I chose to be here, but can I please come home tonight and return in the morning?" I thought nothing of this. It seemed so natural. I simply had a knowing that God existed and that I had come here with a purpose. I innately knew that I had existed elsewhere before being born as Kaye.

Over the years, as an empathic, heart-centered, and sensitive child, I, like so many children, felt like an outsider, different and alone. My nature is to communicate and connect, and I understood the deep workings of others because I had that internal voice always explaining why others did or did not do things, like not being emotionally available. Anger and frustration grew within me. Where did I fit into this world? Although always deeply searching for answers to the bigger questions of life, as a teenager and into my twenties, I no longer felt comfortable using the word "God." Instead, I replaced the word with Spirit. That is until I experienced what I knew to be God one day.

Over my lifespan, from childhood to adulthood, I've experienced numerous accidents. I nearly drowned in the surf once, fell off horses and survived three serious car accidents, it was as if I was punishing myself somehow and trying to leave this painful place and return to where I had come from. So, when a man saved me from drowning in the surf, I felt immense anger as I had reached a sense of peace and surrender that I was about to die. I was only eleven.

I share this briefly because all those experiences led me to where I am today, able to write about "motivating your life."

Because of the first car accident, in which the front of my car met me up close and personal and there was a large tree before me that the police said, "your car should be wrapped around this tree, you are so lucky" I was left with physical pain that no one alleviated. For the first time in my life, I experienced debilitating migraines. Because of this pain and the stress it created, I learned to meditate. This was the beginning of my journey to discover how to motivate my life.

I have spent over three decades supporting others on their journey and even longer remembering myself. What follows is what I now know.

Meditation saved my life. I first learned to meditate with my eyes open and focus on one point. During one of my meditations, I experienced the brightest and whitest pinprick of light across the other side of the room. I blinked a few times, thinking my eyes were playing a trick on me. They were not. This point of light, so intensely bright, shot across the room and into my chest, pushing me backwards; all-encompassing energy of love flowed through me, around me and out from me. I wept from the inner depths of my joy, knowing and a sense of oneness. No words can describe this experience.

No one explained what had taken place. I am not sure why I asked others because I knew that I had experienced God beyond a doubt. Pure love and bright, expansive, all-encompassing light. I was comfortable with what that word meant for me from that day on.

I wanted to keep learning, growing, and understanding. I thought that maybe I had found a place of belonging with like-minded people. What I found was not what I expected, but it turned out to be what I needed. I found facilitators and teachers who were challenged by me and my gift of knowing and inner guidance. I was bullied and alienated, an experience familiar throughout my teenage and adult years. The egoic mind either wants to raise us above others to feel superior or push us down to feel inferior. I do not feel the need to go into this topic in-depth. I only share this snippet for context. These experiences were a blessing. They forced me to continue going within and getting to know and trust this inner voice of knowing more intimately. I also understood ego and the human condition. The experience also ignited my deep, lifelong desire to help support and guide others through the terrain of illusion and develop a strong relationship with their knowing beyond the illusions that intruded, internally and externally.

Handing our power to false stories and beliefs or external people is not motivating. It is suppressing. Discovering the power and potential within is our true source of motivation.

I knew from that moment on that we are all connected and that everything exists within us all. That voice of understanding that had guided and comforted me all my life is a voice we all have! My inner voice of knowing never dimmed, as it does for so many. I suppose that was part of the reason I came here. To support others back to feeling and understanding their inner power. To become self-motivated, leaders of their lives.

Meditation developed my ability to become a witness. I learned to witness my constant thoughts taking my energy. Always back to the past or being fearfully projected into a perceived, however not yet lived, future. The problem was I was never present in the place of nowhere, now here. The present. It is called the present because here the gift lives—a peaceful joy. In the moment of the now, fear, doubts, and insecurities cannot exist.

The unconscious mind is where all the false stories and beliefs gather. Over years of experiences and meaning, we attach to them and the library of what we take on board from others. Family beliefs, society, and the collective history of past generations. This becomes the fuel for the subconscious mind. The subconscious mind says, "Whatever you feed me, I will use to draw this experience to you so you can live out this perception." The subconscious says yes to your unconscious directives.

It only holds this power over you until you become the witness and change your alliance to your superconscious mind—that part of you that is your inner voice of knowing power and potential. Many names can be attributed to this: intuition, God, Spirit, Divine, or Soul. It does not matter which term you use. I have always known my inner voice to be "knowing;" words have power and I find this powerful because knowing is a word of certainty. The dictionary says it means, "in full awareness or consciousness."

The key here is to become conscious of the unconscious and limiting subconscious influences and to place them into the passenger seat of your life as you strengthen your inner voice of knowing and take the wheel. Drive your life. Your Soul is now your compass, no longer the egoic mind in control, keeping you in the past or harpooned to a perceived future. When this is attained, motivation comes from within you. You are leading your life from the inside out.

So, what do I mean about passenger seats and drivers' seats? Most people feel like life is happening to them rather than from them. Fears, doubts, and insecurities often rule how they react to life, with a feeling of powerlessness and overwhelm, victims of their circumstances. This metaphorically places them in the passenger seat or backseat of their life as the deep-seated false stories and beliefs drive their responses to their external circumstances and experiences. Being reactive rather than proactive. Think of it as having a wounded inner child driving your vehicle. When you understand and unmask these false stories and beliefs, releasing the suppressed emotions and pain, realigning with the power and potential within, you take over the driver's seat, navigating the pathways before you with conscious intent. Your inner knowing is your compass as you choose the landscape.

Fears, doubts, insecurities, and limitations are no longer at the wheel of your life. Instead, they are moved to the passenger seat as

9

you finally take control with your knowing, acting as the conscious creator of your life. Deserving, understanding, connection, purpose, and insight are your fuel.

Inner motivation is powerful. Yes, you can go to seminars and workshops, read, or listen to books or YouTube and come away feeling amped up and ready to conquer the world. However, if you don't do the real work, the continual application of what is required for the transfer of power, that feeling will disappear as fast as it was ignited. That's because it was fueled by an outside source that pumped up your egoic mind. Developing and maintaining the power of self-motivation involves daily practice in removing the charge from those old beliefs that hold toxic and limiting feelings.

That is why meditation is the first foundation for witnessing and harnessing, aside from all its other benefits.

The voice of knowing within the heart knows what path you need to take and what decisions you need to make to live a life you love and to achieve the results you seek, following your Soul's purpose. It knows the power and potential that reside within you. This voice is the voice of your future self that has achieved what you aspire to, calling to you, "Come, you are already successful; I have walked the path before you. Let me show you the way." *This voice is your greatest supporter and knows you better than you know yourself!*

Physics tells us that matter comprises molecules and that even something solid, such as a table, is vibrating all the time; we are no different. We are energy. Most people do not know what their energy feels like due to being affected by everyone else's energy. The thoughts and feelings you experience may not even be your own! So, to know your energy, you must clear yourself so you can feel it properly. This will help you 'sense' the voice of knowing within your heart center unencumbered by other influences.

This is the process of cutting your cords:

- Set this as your intention.

- Start with a few deep breaths through the nose, push the breath down to the base of the spine and then release the breath out the mouth, dropping the jaw.

- Call all energies before you that are connected to you, other than yours, clamp both ends, and cut the cords. Then, do the same process again, calling all energies to you from behind this time.

- Allow your whole body and being to be bathed in a brilliant bluish-white light of transformation. This is a cleansing process, so you are now clear of other influences and can sense or feel what your energy feels like.

I like to do this process when I am in the shower since it takes no extra time from my day; in addition, the water makes it easy to visualize the light flowing over and through me.

This is only a suggestion. You can adapt this routine to suit you and the imagery you relate to best. What is important is the intention. For example, I do not clamp the cords. Instead, I call upon a flaming sword of Truth to cut the threads swiftly and cleanly as the flame seals the ends. Connecting and cutting or using the sword of Truth is final, so the energy does not continue to leak. When a baby is born, we clamp the cord!

I recommend starting your day and finishing your day with this process. You don't want to take your boss and co-workers' energy to bed with you, do you? I also use this process if I feel emotional; sometimes the emotion quickly disappears because it was not mine – I was affected by someone else. The more you do this practice, the more you can feel when another energy encroaches. It improves your clarity of thought about becoming familiar with that inner voice of knowing.

It takes time and experience to strengthen and develop trust, like any good relationship. The same applies to allowing yourself to be guided by your inner knowing.

Here is how I experience my inner knowing.

- It's a voice inside me. It sounds like me yet speaks to me. It has a full-body feeling, unlike negative talk felt more in the head because it comes from false stories and beliefs.

- Sudden insight while being busy. Sitting on the toilet, vacuuming the house, or getting ready in the morning, it just comes up from within or smacks you between the eyes. If you don't recognize it the first time, it will keep nudging. If you ignore it, please act by the third nudge, so the nudge doesn't turn into a kick up the arse. One of my car accidents was a kick-up-the-arse moment to force me to make a move I knew I needed to but was avoiding. No kidding.

- When you feel like moving in a particular direction and it excites you, the feeling is often followed by fear. Yes, that is correct. The fear is your friend showing up to say, "Now you must grow and let go of something." When you know and understand this, it excites you because it is a sure sign. I once attended an information night and by the end, I knew that I would be coached by the facilitator. First I felt the excitement and then the fear. My knowing told me I wasn't going to do the less expensive group coaching option. My knowing told me to go all in and invest in the one-on-one. It was one of the most powerful and transformative decisions I have made, and that coach is now an excellent friend.

- Signs are another way our inner knowing can communicate with us. Lyrics in a song, something read in a book, or something someone says to us. It stands out and we feel it within. I was driving my car one day and listening to an audiobook. There was a chapter where the author spoke first, getting herself a coach to transform her life. Bam. I knew instantly that I needed to invest in myself and get a coach. I thought it would help me build a multi-level marketing business that could lead me back into coaching. After one session, it had become one hundred percent clear that it needed to be flipped around. I found myself back in the business of coaching and healing again, with my multi-level marketing ticking away in the background.

The key is not to have any expectations when guided by your inner knowing. Expectations are limitations that can lead to disappointment; something not happening how you want it to or in the time frame you want—the "how" is not your business. Sit back, keep your hands on the wheel and follow that inner compass. This is where the feeling of magic, synchronicity, and flow exists. I have a saying: "I cannot see around corners. Only God has the full picture." (Remember, you can replace the word God with whatever suits your perspective.)

Another saying I live by repeatedly proves its power is this: "Only goodness comes from the Universe, even if I cannot see it at the time." I recall one such time when I had to align myself with this statement. I had left my first husband and recently moved from a beautiful ten-acre property into a rented house near my three children's school. As you can imagine, it was a challenging and emotional time, and no sooner had we moved than it looked like I would have to move myself and the children again because the owner wanted to sell. Did I feel stress and fear? Absolutely I did. An emotion took hold and then I stopped and aligned with what I knew. I breathed, meditated, cleared, and aligned by repeating the statement repeatedly until it embedded in me with feeling.

While focused on the statement, there was no room for what-ifs and why me, projected fears. My inner knowing told me that everything would work out. After events so beautifully unexpected and aligned, I discovered just how little the owner had paid for the house. I followed my guidance and made an offer, which he accepted because he needed a fast sale—sold for a bargain! Was it my dream house? No. But, it was security for my children and myself that came at a bargain price and I could have sold it the next day for more. It was a stepping-stone to bigger aspirations.

Imagine the energy I would have wasted had I stayed in fear and victimhood. Stress is going against the grain. Being in flow is like the river that flows over and around obstacles and, eventually, wears down a mighty rock! I couldn't see around the corners; however, my voice of knowing my compass and my decision to choose my perception and response was in my hands. The universe was not contriving against me; it aligned my future with me.

In my journey, I have learned that perceptions are created by the beliefs, false stories, and emotions stored within us. These beliefs, stories and feelings can be released to reveal a higher truth and purpose, altering our perception. The Truth is beyond the shadow of our belief systems.

Here is what has moved me through many challenging situations:

- Journeying into the heart of situations to uncover the gift it gave me. I asked myself, "Why did I need to have this experience?" Or "how does this serve me?" I call these power questions because when asked with the power of intention to release and recover, they call up a response.

- Applying love, compassion, understanding and forgiveness to all experiences, people, and myself.

I am not saying that insights and freedom come instantly. It's always a work in progress and the more you apply, the more adept you become, and the faster you move through to the other side. It took years for the pain, hurt, anger, and disconnect to take root, so it would take time, dedication, and effort to develop a new way of being, which became the new norm. Why does it? Because the more you remember the genuine, authentic you, the freer you feel, the happier you are, and the more empowered you become. You live a life you love that is more connected and expansive than you initially imagined. You are the leader within your life and your creation. Now that is motivating!

I have been through a lot in life (haven't we all?). Accidents and injuries, emotionally unavailable caregivers and partners, sexual violation of trust, exclusion, betrayal, wrongly judged, bullied by people close and in positions of authority, and abuse. I even had times when I was financially challenged. But this chapter is not about what has happened to me or where I was. It is about what I did to change it and what motivated me. Challenges hit us all and the sooner we come to recognize this, the more connected and compassionate we will become. It is not about what has happened. It is about how you will respond.

The power question is this: Does my response create the feeling and life I deserve, the life I love? Does it make me feel good about myself, or lead to self-loathing? Am I being proactive or reactive? Reactive is saying you are responding from some deep-seeded experience that created a belief and story within that needs to be explored and addressed. Reactive has an emotional charge. Proactive is changing your way of seeing things and acting from new beliefs, calmly responding to reduce negative impact. Why? Because you are worthy of an incredible life and having that starts with you. When you make that choice, you are respecting yourself. No one else will respect you if you don't gift it to yourself first. Remember, change takes time and consistency until it becomes the new normal. We are all human and perfectly imperfect at times.

What motivated me to cultivate a new way of being and doing was the thought of the end of my life. I didn't want to live with regrets and self-loathing, I didn't want to feel powerless, I didn't want to be internally unhappy, and I did not want to have life just happen. I wanted to be at the helm of my life and give it a damn good go.

I wanted my children to have a courageous example. One of my daughters created a new way of spelling this word, Kayerageous, which was a huge compliment. I would never say, "What would have happened if?" at the end of my life. I was prepared to fall short, knowing I had given it all. The thing is, the more you go within, the more you listen to that inner voice. When you receive the support and develop the skills to weed your inner garden and feel allowed and deserving, life unfolds more magnificently – often in the most creative and unexpected ways. In short, I wanted to be happy regardless of external circumstances! So, I made a choice.

Including meditation, here is what I did and still do:

- Practiced conscious breathing.

- Witnessing my inner dialogue and spending it on something more empowering. I created statements that started with I AM. Anything starting with I AM has power to it. The I AM is the Source within you.

- I wrote down my thoughts, feelings, and aspirations.

- I practiced daily gratitude and appreciation. What you appreciate, appreciates.

- I witnessed my spoken words so I could change them to more positive words. From what I call below-the-line to above-the-line language.

- Anytime I had a negative thought or word, I said to myself, "I cancel that out and I forgive myself;" then I replaced it with the new.

- When shit (challenges) happened, I aligned to firmer beliefs because shit will either stink up a place or fertilize a garden. The garden is my life.

- I learned how to say no and set boundaries.

- I gave myself time. To meditate, soak in a bath, go for a walk, dance, or call a girlfriend. Whatever made me feel topped up, nurtured, and happy.

- I invested in myself and my personal growth.

- I learned how to forgive. First, you need a genuine intention and desire to forgive. Forgiveness is the gift of freedom we give ourselves. It claims back energy from a person or situation.

- I put up statements and images that kept my focus and fed my subconscious.

- I applied love, compassion, understanding and forgiveness to myself and others. That can take time, so recognizing it can be a work in progress.

- I learned how to let go of people who no longer reflected the improved me. We are each like an individual note on a piano; we are all beautiful. But some notes harmonize together, and others do not. As we transform and grow, we change our resonance.

- I learned that I am not too much or too loud and that I don't talk too much. I liked my unique and eclectic self. It's none of my business what another person says or thinks about me, only what I say and think about myself.

- If feeling anxious or emotional, I place my hand on my chest, tap lightly, and say *love, compassion, understanding and forgiveness*. It connects awareness to the heart's intelligence. It's calming and centering.

The process is a little like learning to drive a car. First, you must think about it, clutch in, change gear, accelerate and then one day, you go without thinking about it. It has become an integrated process.

Conscious breathing is when you breathe through the nose, following that breath down to the base of the spine, holding the breath and then releasing it through the mouth, dropping the jaw and opening wide (not with pursed lips). This style of deep breathing connects us to ourselves and our feelings. It's a deep, connected breath. Most people are shallow breathing in life. This breathing can also release emotions. Ask yourself where you feel the emotion in the body and then breathe into where it is, for example, the throat. The energy associated with the feeling will move in the body. Keep breathing into it until it eventually lifts and leaves the body. It will also help you to know your deepest needs. When you know your deepest needs, you can then say no as required and set clear boundaries to honour yourself. I used to be an instant yes girl. Unconsciously it was to ensure people loved me, even if it meant depleting and ignoring my needs. I would walk around the house expressing different ways to say no! When asked something of me to break the old habit, I would say, "I will get back to you on that." It would allow me to check in with myself to see if it's in my best interest.

Whenever we go through change and move beyond our comfort zone, fears will rise. It's a sure sign that growth is required. If you try to suppress the fears, they will get louder. Ignore them, and they will take hold and stifle you. I face my fears by writing them down with the title these are my fears. They are not my truth. Underneath the written fears, I write these were my fears. They are no longer my truth and then I would write my empowered truth and finish my writing. These are my truth. This process diffuses the fears.

One chapter is not enough to communicate to you the whole extent of my journey, but I have given you the best overall guidance I can and supported you towards your inner motivation and power that exists within.

Let me finish with this: If you want permanent motivation, a motivation not reliant on outside sources and stimulation then go within, tune in to your knowing. It's there to guide and support you. The inner knowing will never abandon you. It will always be your compass throughout your life, no matter what it brings before you. Your consistent companion, champion, and guide is the inner voice of knowing, power, and potential.

The knowing is the Source, the power is Soul, and the potential is your future self. The trinity becomes one powerful force of inner motivation and fulfillment.

"The power of change is in your hands."

"Create the highest, grandest vision possible for your life, because you become what you believe."

~ Oprah Winfrey

CHAPTER TWO

Creating Lasting Motivation

By Jamie Fair

In this chapter, I intend to give you the skills, knowledge, and techniques to create monumental, cumulative, and self-sustaining levels of motivation. By applying what you're about to learn, it is my sincerest belief you will progress from wherever you are to a fulfilling future packed with new possibilities. Furthermore, you will leverage ever-increasing self-motivation to overcome any obstacles between you and what you want.

Increased motivation can be leveraged to quit smoking, lose weight, commit to exercising, start a new relationship, end an abusive one, land a new job or leave a dead-end one, chase promotion or switch careers, run a charity, or start a business. Whatever you want from the endless possibilities that life offers, you can use what you learn in this chapter to fulfill that desire and live your life to the fullest.

You're going to learn how to create motivation, and how to generate enough drive to keep going. You will realize that you are capable of consistent and growing motivation to repeatedly break through barriers. When you do, you'll wonder where else you've been holding yourself back and start to seek new experiences.

Maybe you've only dared hope that life can be whatever you want. I'm going to show you it's not only possible but probable for you. If you are willing to put in the time with the processes I outline, your life can be better than you can imagine!

You may be familiar with a few of these techniques and might even have tried some. If that's the case, I encourage you to read this information as if for the first time. Come at it with a learner's mind. Perhaps you will hear it differently and it will hit home for you. Understand that while each technique alone has the power to shift your life, the real power comes from combining them.

Are you ready to create lasting motivation? Let's get started!

Push Until You Feel Called

To make a change, you can't just sit around waiting for motivation to strike. Motivation comes from identifying your wants and aspirations. When you want something, you create the motivation to seek it—the greater the desire, the more intense the motivation generated.

Getting your motivation started can sometimes be a challenge. It may feel like you're pushing a boulder or a stalled car. Since motivation is created by action, you must keep going. Even if you're weary, don't give up. Your vehicle will pick up momentum. Gradually, pushing becomes easier, and soon you'll find that you're hardly pushing at all. A body in motion stays in motion and it won't be long before it's sustaining itself. Then all you have to do is steer!

To begin, we need something that excites you. So, let's walk through an exercise to find that for you.

What Excites You?

Start by listing things that excite you. What are your areas of interest? What have you done in the past, or what would you like to do that would light you up? What could you create, do, give, or be that sparks something inside?

Make your list first, then we're going to perform a brief but powerful exercise. Clients are often amazed at what comes up for them. It's a great way to uncover what generates excitement and hidden interests!

Begin by getting yourself into a state of calm and relaxation. Remove yourself from all distractions and close your eyes. Take ten deep, slow breaths focusing on only the inhalation and the exhalation. Then, ask yourself a question from that centered place. What would you do if you knew with absolute certainty, to the very fiber of your being, that you would succeed?

Set aside all thoughts of your present circumstances and history. Let go of thoughts of needing to keep it real. This is about finding what lights you up. Remember to approach this with the mindset you'll succeed no matter what. You're going to win, overcome, create, or be a master of whatever you can imagine yourself doing. What would you dare to dream?

If you come up with something and feel your heart flutter with fear, you've found what genuinely excites you! If fear comes up, explore it further. Write that one down and go after it! Fear is an excellent indicator of something we want to do but hold ourselves back from pursuing. That is an ideal place from which to build your motivation.

Add whatever comes up for you to your list!

Imagine What You Want

Now that we've got our creativity and excitement flowing let's take the next step. We do that by picturing ourselves doing that thing that excites us. Our minds can create strong feelings from simply imagining doing something. This is because our brains can't distinguish between something happening in real life and something we vividly picture.

Go back to that centered state. Close your eyes and imagine what it would be like doing that thing that excites or scares you. Picture yourself as if it's already happening. Project yourself into that moment. Use the incredible power of your mind to see yourself stepping into that future you. What is that version of you thinking about? What are they talking about? What are they feeling? Be fully in that moment.

Experience what you want as if it's already happening. By doing this, you are programming your mind to move you toward that dream. You are priming your subconscious to look for opportunities to create that reality and increasing your motivation to head in that direction. Repeat this often. The image you are creating will soon propel you forward!

Motivation Deterrents

Before we attempt to tackle motivating ourselves to even higher degrees, let's cover what blocks our motivation and how we can overcome those barriers.

From my life experience, and from what I've observed when helping others, three things top the list of motivation blockers. These are: overwhelm, criticism and fear. So, let's deep dive into each.

Dealing With Overwhelm

Have you ever chosen to pursue a significant goal only to feel deflated when you realize what it will take? We look at what's required and out goes our motivation, only to be replaced by an urge to run and hide. It suddenly feels as though the thing we want is just too daunting. We know hiding won't get us anywhere, but any attempt to go after what we want is just too much and we feel overwhelmed. We've all experienced this sensation. Let's look at ways we can conquer it!

If your boss came up to you and told you that you had to complete 50 steps of this and do 18 things you've never done before and four things that require you to step out of your comfort zone, you'd probably feel like quitting. When we set our sights on a lofty goal and see all that's going to be required to reach it, we have those same feelings. No wonder we struggle to get started!

Our natural inclination will be to start the beat down on ourselves. However, we must avoid doing that, as it will only make conquering the task more difficult. Instead, try just acknowledging how you feel. Realize that it's understandable and to be expected. It's okay to feel overwhelmed.

Getting started in the face of this feeling is like climbing a peak. Instead of looking at the entire mountain, look at the trail directly in front of you. The whole mountain may be daunting, but you can easily tackle a few hundred yards of trail. When you get done with that segment, celebrate and only then look at combating the next stretch of track.

Think of it like building Ikea™ furniture or a Lego™ set. Break it down into smaller pieces. Is there a segment you could see yourself attempting? Find one small step you can take and take it. Once you've completed that single step, no matter how small, **acknowledge yourself!** I cannot stress the importance of this component. If you only recognize your efforts after completing the entire challenge, you're self-sabotaging. Instead, keep taking it a step at a time, acknowledging yourself at the end of each.

As silly as it may sound, recognize the small wins! We get a little dopamine hit every time we check off a to-do item. So, make sure your big tasks are broken down into smaller ones and check each off thus creating cumulative wins and steadily increasing your feel-good chemicals. Celebrating after any effort is so important; we will cover this in more detail later.

Additionally, each step is an opportunity to learn something new! We're creating growth and motivation!

Criticism Is The Motivation Killer

Imagine you have a huge garden full of weeds and you take on removing the overgrowth. You're out there giving it your all, sweating like crazy. It's back-breaking work and takes all day. You finally stop, stand back, and survey your efforts. The garden was a disaster and now looks fantastic! Excitedly, you grab your partner to show them. Instead of recognizing any of your great work, they point out what you didn't do, how you missed a spot, and how you damaged one plant. They go on and on about what you did wrong.

That doesn't feel good, does it? Plus, how likely are you to want to put in that effort again? Unfortunately, we frequently criticize our efforts in similar ways. Criticism is a motivation killer of the worst kind.

Most of us have an internal voice that flogs us severely if we don't do what we said we would do. It usually sounds something like, "I can't believe I didn't get that done. I'm such a _____," and insert something so awful we would never say it to anyone else.

It's not okay we talk to ourselves in this way, and we've got to put a stop to it. When you self-criticize, even if you're not consciously aware of it, some part of you feels just like that gardener and it destroys future motivation.

Rather than resorting to being cruel to yourself, try to put a positive spin on the situation. For example, instead of calling yourself "lazy," tell yourself, "I'll reprioritize to fit this in my schedule." Instead of telling yourself, "I suck at this!" say, "I'll give it another try." Instead of, "It's too hard," say, "I'll attempt this from another angle."

Consider what you would suggest to a loved one or a dear friend in the same situation. I hear almost unanimously, "I would tell them to go easier on themselves." When we step back and see through the lens of love, it shifts our perspective. We all try harder than we acknowledge. We rarely give ourselves credit for our progress, and we are way too hard on ourselves.

Instead of criticizing yourself, try being your advocate. Treat yourself like you would a loved one!

Pushing On Your Fears

The biggest obstacle to motivation is fear. Fear can stop us cold. We may be driven to do something, but if fear exceeds our motivation, it's unlikely to happen. Yet, if we take the right steps, we can push through the fear of any kind.

Most of us see fears as insurmountable walls – barriers we can't knock down. I want to assure you that any fear can be neutralized, overcome, or made manageable. We get there by pushing on those fears often, even if it's just in a small, incremental way. We can erode any wall if we keep picking away at it. Maybe it's a grain of sand one day and an entire section of wall the next – what matters is that you just keep pushing. Keep tearing down that wall a little at a time.

Perhaps you've been to the Stratosphere in Las Vegas. If you fear heights, that's an ideal place to push on that fear. I remember riding the elevator and having hard-core regrets I'd agreed to go. I vividly recall figuring out how I could stay in the elevator, hoping no one would notice. I can still remember feeling panic as the floor count on the elevator display skyrocketed upwards. I didn't lean on the glass as I saw others do, but I did go outside onto the observation deck, where I could feel the sway of the building in the wind.

Terrifying as that experience was, I took out a big chunk of that fear. That massive wall, for me, was marginally smaller than it was the day before. I moved the needle that day and I continue to do so.

Conquering Your Fears

I want to encourage you to push on your fears because the truth is that they're not going to move independently. They will stay exactly as they are and never change unless you act. Who knows, you may discover, as I did about public speaking, that one of your greatest gifts is on the other side of that fear!

It may not be easy, but I promise you this works. Once you push over that first fear wall, it will change your life. Because once you push down that wall, you can see the possibilities that lie beyond it. They were always there, but you could never see them. Once you conquer your fears, you will see your life in a whole new light, and you'll feel motivated to keep going.

Now it's your turn. First, write down your top two to four fears, then list ways you could push on them.

Where could your motivation take you if fear didn't stop you?

Embracing The Fearful Aspect

We all have a part of us inside afraid to reach for something greater. This part of us wants us to keep our heads down and play it safe. It fears anything that might be challenging or that sets us apart.

In fairness, that part of us has the best of intentions. Its job is to keep us from making mistakes, being embarrassed, or tasting failure. This well-intending part of our psyche tries to keep us small. It constantly tries to fit in and only feels relaxed when we do nothing outside our comfort zone.

Its favorite method of doing this is via "what if." It will explain why we shouldn't move outside our comfort zones. "What if you fail?" "What if you can't do it?" "What if you're not good enough?"

Well-meaning as it may be, it negates motivation. If we accept its argument, we go along with that fearfulness. By agreeing with it, by choosing not to pursue a goal, we strengthen that part of us that keeps us down. When we act from fear, we reinforce fear. For many, that voice of fear becomes the loudest and most followed.

This part of us will utilize our memories and entire emotional history to get its way. If one "what if" doesn't work, it will find another. If those don't work, it will pull from awful memories of the past to remind us of what could happen. It has an arsenal to throw at us and it is relentless.

We struggle to counter this force that wants to keep us stagnant. So, what can we do against something that can throw our deepest, darkest weaknesses at us?

The first strategy is to reverse the what-if scenarios. When the inner voice comes up with the "What if I fail?" question, thank it and counter with "What if I succeed?" Amp it up! "What if it turns out to be better than expected?" "What if I succeed beyond my wildest imagination?" "What if this is the start of something incredible?" If you throw out a series of positive potential outcomes every time the negative what-ifs come up, that negative part of you will quickly lose power!

The second and even more effective strategy is to see it for what it is. Despite how it appears, this aspect of our psyche is not our enemy. Imagine a parent yelling at you for doing something unsafe. If you grasp they were just worried about you, you can see past the yelling and hear the loving message behind it. You can deflate its force when you understand that the fear and the what-ifs are coming from a place of concern.

Most of us have learned to habitually deal with these fears either by suppressing them or by going to war with them. Unfortunately, neither of these is a long-term winning tactic. Suppressing feelings only causes them to come back even stronger and battling with that part of ourselves only increases internal tension.

29

Perhaps surprisingly, the answer lies in appreciation and love. We can acknowledge and give gratitude to that fearful aspect of ourselves. It's only doing its job. Although the outcome of its efforts detracts from our lives, in its way, it cares about us. Let us meet its care with gratitude and grace.

Imagine that fearful aspect of you as a scared child. That child has been hurt before and is trying to prevent that from happening again. Rather than yelling at this child, which will only frustrate them and cause them to shout louder, treat them with kindness. They want to be heard, so acknowledge them. "Thank you so much for trying to keep me safe. I acknowledge you are scared right now." See the concern behind the fear. Once you do, you will perceive an immediate decrease in intensity and the voice will grow quieter.

These may seem like unusual strategies but try them. You'll see for yourself the effectiveness of acknowledgement, and, through practice, it will become easier and habitual. The next time you try to motivate yourself and the fears and what-ifs come up, see them for what they are. Give gratitude to them for trying to keep you safe, and from that place, press on.

Small Decisions Matter

Now that we've explored the things that hold us back from feeling motivated and how to overcome them, let's work on creating sustained motivation. The first step is to stick to your decisions.

Are you the person that hits the snooze button when the alarm goes off? Consider that the night before, you decided that was the ideal wake-up time, yet your first decision of the day is to ignore that decision! It seems trivial, like no big thing, but I proffer it *is* significant. This is huge in all areas where we fall short of our commitments.

Failure to see our commitments through adds up. While each event alone may seem inconsequential, they are like grains of sand. Enough of them can change the course of a river. By continually failing to meet our commitments, that's what we're doing. We're creating a pathway in our minds. Soon it becomes easier and easier to follow that same path of not following through. We strengthen a neural pathway that says, "I don't do what I say I'll do."

So, let's change this! From this point forward, I want you to do everything in your power to stick with your commitments, whether to yourself or others. Become the person that does what you say you will do *every time*. If you intend to go to the gym after work, even if you work late, make it happen. If you tell yourself you need to stop by the store on your way home, but the commute goes long, go to the store. Be very careful what you commit to and stay true to your word. Build up that mental muscle you do what you say, especially to yourself!

Rewarding Success

While we touched on rewards in a previous section, this is so important we'll cover it now in more detail.

We've all been raised in a system. Somewhere in our past, our ancestors discovered that they could get animals to follow a particular behavior through rewards and punishments. Those same people used that system on their children and saw success and so it continued generation after generation. Most of us had parents that rewarded us for good behavior and punished us for bad. Nearly all of us parented our children this way. Most teachers use a reward system. Let's face it, completing tasks to earn a reward has been hardwired into us.

Let's leverage this to create sustained motivation! For example, suppose you have a daunting project you're dreading. Yet despite your dread, you put in the effort and make it happen. Rather than briefly acknowledging yourself before moving on to the next thing, what if you handle it differently? What if you recognize that effort? Perhaps you buy something you've been denying yourself or do something fun you wouldn't normally do. Maybe you pick up a cool new gadget or spend some quality time with a friend.

Because we've all been brought up this way, rewarding yourself affects how your mind perceives challenges. You'll be slightly more motivated to tackle a problematic task the next time. Consider what happens if you *keep* consistently rewarding yourself. Every time you do something difficult, you reward yourself equally in scope to the undertaking. That is how we capitalize on this built-in system.

Can you see how this method creates increasing motivation? *Take the time to reward yourself.* As time goes on, that cumulative drive will snowball your motivation into momentum!

Momentum

The most effective means of creating sustained motivation is through momentum. We need momentum! We want to create so much steam that even our fears won't be able to stop us. We want to build up so much velocity we can motivate ourselves to accomplish things well beyond our comfort levels.

Start small and leverage the rewarding success method. Find some little task you know you can quickly get done. After completion, celebrate in a meaningful way, then bring another small objective to fruition, and again, celebrate your small win. Repeat this behavior a few dozen times. Get a bunch of wins under your belt while creating a self-rewarding habit. Only once you've reached that point should you go after something more challenging. Reward yourself when you do it, but this time in a slightly bigger way. Then do another more difficult task. Again, celebrate your win. Repeat this pattern and keep scaling up. You will be amazed at the results!

If you hit upon an undertaking and find your motivation lagging, then stop. That's an indication you haven't built up enough momentum to push through challenges at that level yet. Instead, leverage one method you've learned: break it up into smaller segments or go back down a notch in difficulty where you were succeeding and do more.

This is a gradual process. Be patient with yourself. You're rewriting neural pathways and the secrets to success here are starting small and repetition. Through repetition, we build momentum and change our self-image. We see ourselves as someone motivated and driven to do hard things through repeatedly winning.

Create positive forward momentum. That's the key. Do it day after day until it feels easy, then do it more. Build up that snowball effect. Leverage that force that moves with so much power it will smash through any obstacle!

Failure Is Just An Experience

My wife and I were attending an online Zen class. The exercise was to deeply examine topics from the perspectives of both for and against. Regardless of our stance, we were asked to dive deep into both sides of our chosen subject. We then had to speak from each perspective and openly share how it felt. The final exercise was to speak from a perspective neither for nor against – a place that isn't interested in taking sides.

We split up into small groups to decide on what topic we wanted to discuss. I had an insight we should dive into success and failure. The rest agreed.

As we spoke about success, it went as you would expect. From this perspective, we had a preference to win. Failure was not an option. Someone pointed out that a desire for success can frequently be detrimental; some want success so badly that they sacrifice essential relationships to pursue it.

Next, we approached failure. We each thought about what it would be like to prefer failure. As we went around, we shared statements like, "Failure is a chance to learn," "If all we get is success, we don't learn anything," and "It's from failure that we adapt and grow."

Lastly, we shifted to the perspective of neither for nor against – being okay with either. From this vantage, we were able to see that we label success as "good" and failure as "bad," but regardless of the outcome, both are merely experiences. Failure doesn't indicate we are somehow intrinsically lesser or incapable.

I want you to have this direct experience. Do this independently or find a partner or two to make it more interesting. Start by taking the perspective of being for success and against failure – our usual stance. Take turns saying a few statements from that mindset for three to four minutes. Then switch and try to put yourself in the mind of someone for failure and against success. It may not be easy at first, but you'll find our minds are fluid and able to hold alternative perspectives. Lastly, adopt a mindset neither for nor against. What if you were above all of that? How do success and failure look, then?

You may understand that failure is just an experience, but it's profound to have a direct understanding of yourself. If you do the exercise, you'll comprehend that failure isn't something to be feared or avoided. Instead, you'll discover that failure is just another part of the human experience. You'll likely find, as we did, that failure is preferred because that's where the growth is!

When you can let go of your fear of failure, you'll feel more motivated to pursue a life that excites and challenges you. You will be free to go after experiences you might otherwise have avoided. Embracing failure can motivate you to welcome even more of life!

Taskmaster Or Coach?

Imagine having a job where your boss is upbeat and inspires you to do your best. When you do something well, they sing your praises! They may leave notes of appreciation or talk about your excellent work in front of others. When you do poorly, they tell you, "I've got your back," It's all good," or, "You're learning, and you've got this!" No matter how much you mess up, they aren't dissuaded. They never talk badly about you. Instead, they believe in you and demonstrate it in little ways each day. You would likely want to do more for this person. They would inspire your loyalty and motivate you to want to do even better. With them, you would feel safe and be willing to try hard things. For them, you would strive to be your best.

Now imagine working for someone where nothing is ever good enough. If you succeed, they might mention it, but praise is short-lived. You could work all night getting a project done for them and they barely acknowledge you. As soon as you learn one assignment, it's on to the next harder one with scarcely a nod. When you mess up, they berate you. They can't believe you messed up again. Finally, they ask, "Are you ever going to get this right?"

That does not inspire loyalty. That person isn't someone you'll go over and above for. Every assignment will feel like drudgery and the harder the task, the more you'll dread it because no amount of work will make them happy or earn you acknowledgement. This kind of boss destroys motivation.

I've got an important question to ask you. Which kind of boss are you? I don't mean to others. *Which kind of boss are you to yourself?* When you do something difficult, do you take the time to praise yourself, or do you barely acknowledge what you did and it's on to the next thing? When you make a mistake, do you tell yourself, "I'll get this next time!" or do you berate yourself? I'm sure you can see the correlation between how you treat yourself and whether you're creating positive or negative momentum. Correspondingly, are you creating motivation and loyalty in yourself, or are you detracting from your efforts?

Are you encouraging or discouraging yourself? Are you a coach to yourself or a taskmaster? Most of us have been taskmasters with little regard for the long-term impact of this pattern of behavior. If that's you, it's time to turn that around. To build maximum motivation, be your advocate. See yourself as both boss and employee. Treat yourself as if you were the most important person in the world. Shower yourself with praise.

Acknowledge and express gratitude for your efforts. Those other facets inside you will be far more amenable to doing hard things!

Conclusion

Motivation doesn't just strike. If someone proclaims they don't feel motivated, they aren't putting forth the effort to produce it. To feel the fire of motivation in our lives, we must create a spark! Motivation is generated through the anticipation of pursuing a dream or an exciting possible future. Sustained motivation comes from the intentional application of actions that fan those sparks into flames.

Belief is the final ingredient. By applying what you've learned, you can create all the drive and motivation you will ever need. Believe you can leverage your motivation to move in any direction. Have the certainty you can and will achieve what excites you in life.

Now it's up to you! You have the power to create a future of your choosing. Your destiny is in your hands. Set your sails for a fortune your old self would envy seeing!

Keep feeding that fire!

"Life will only change when you become more committed to your dreams than you are to your comfort zone."

~ Billy Cox

CHAPTER THREE

━━━━━ ∘⟨≈⟩∘ ━━━━━

Unleash Your Hero from Within

By Anthony Dierickx

T hink of your favorite hero or heroine, the one you look up to for motivation. They could be from a famous narrative in a book, T.V. series, movie, or documentary. Maybe you have imagined how it would feel to be like that character, to stand up for what they hold dear. For me, motivational figures have always been those who value freedom, like William Wallace in the iconic movie *Braveheart*, who saves his fellow Scottish countrymen and women from the tyranny of English rule back in the late 13th and early 14th centuries. But heroes are not only found in fiction or history. In my life, I look up to my mother, who's been a source of motivation with her real-estate business, Smart Home Vision, building it from the bottom up and overcoming so many obstacles in her life to achieve this dream. So, let your imagination go wild and find that hero within that you aspire to be!

No matter where we find them, our heroes can serve as examples that help to motivate us to achieve goals in our life. But motivation means nothing without action. Heroes inspire us because they made what seemed impossible possible. The documentary *14 Peaks: Nothing Is Impossible* tells the story of a Nepalese mountaineer, Nirmal Puja, and his team as they attempt to climb all 14 "eight-thousander" peaks in under seven months, including the highest mountain in the world, Mount Everest, which stands at about 8.8km above sea level. This reminds me of the quote by Norman Vincent Peale, "Shoot for the moon. Even if you miss, you'll land among the stars!" Nirmal's story tells us that anything is possible if you set your mind to it.

I've written a few Big Hairy Audacious Goals (BHAG) down in my lifetime; things I never thought were possible to achieve until I coupled them with a hundred percent belief, motivation and faith. One example of that has been my travel experiences in different parts of the world, such as France, Thailand, Fiji, Malaysia, Indonesia, Hong Kong, and China, to name a few, and there is more traveling on the horizon.

Ultimately, I have reached these goals through small collective actions. Darren Hardy goes into detail about this concept in his book *The Compounding Effect*. It's about taking daily cumulative actions that help you achieve your overarching vision for your life. These actions fall like pebbles in a pond, with the ripples being felt across the water's entire surface.

In some shape or form, haven't we all secretly thought about what it would be like to experience our hero's lives in the "real world"? Well, what if I told you, you can, and that I will share a few strategies to show you how?

This chapter will provide you with a snapshot of my journey. I'll share my struggles to give you the belief that if I can do it, you can! It's been a 30-plus-year adventure to reach the level of faith and trust I have today, to set my wings free and soar far and high like a bald eagle, going to places I never thought possible. I've noticed one thing is sure in life – change. We will inevitably grow through changing perspectives that lead to paradigm shifts in how we view our world. This is especially relevant with how fast technological advancements are moving. That's why it's so important we stay anchored in our motivations – our reasons for chasing the dreams we chase.

My childhood began in the dusty iron ore mining town of Whyalla in South Australia. Besides the layers of red dust everywhere, my childhood recollections up to six years old were relatively peaceful since I had a loving and supportive family. I remember spending many days with my family eating fresh fruit from my French grandparents' fruit trees in their backyard garden. You can't have a European ethnic family without fruit trees? Am I right?

Later in life, I was glad to say farewell to Whyalla when we moved to wine country in the Barossa Valley. I didn't miss the red ochre dust and tumbleweeds rolling by. Though, living in regional parts of South Australia, I did come to appreciate the friendliness and close community connections, like, going for a walk down the main street of Tanunda with a "G'day" here and there to passers-by as I walked to pick up a magazine from my local news agency. As I've grown older, I have learned to appreciate the small things in life by taking hold of them and showing gratitude daily. A motivated and abundance mindset is seeded with appreciation rituals instead of being stuck in the familiar and taking it for granted. If you understand that concept and practice it daily, you can have so much more in your life. However, remember to add a spice of belief, flavors of faith, and splashes of action to the mix.

I went to Nuriootpa High School in the Barossa Valley during my teenage years and thoroughly enjoyed my time there. The teachers and my peers were a supportive and connected community drawn from diverse backgrounds. Reminiscing with my school friends when I recently attended my 20-year high school reunion at the old Vine Inn pub in Nuriootpa brought home the importance of our Latin school motto, "Per Aspera Ad Astra," meaning "Through Adversity to the Stars." We will all go through growing pains in our lifetime, and we can either give up or break out to reach the stars and beyond. We're not alone on this journey. My school reunion reminded me of sharing your struggles. You can touch another person's life to motivate them spread their wings and soar high to achieve what they want. Seeing others reach for their goals should motivate us to help them because the success of one of us means the success of all. The humility of servitude is a great gift we can share with our communities that help to sharpen iron with iron. I challenge you to put some time aside to volunteer in an area you are passionate about. I guarantee you will see your world flourish like the Japanese cherry blossom tree. I have fond memories of volunteering my time for 12-plus months with Riding for the Disabled. It was a fantastic experience where you saw autistic kids gain courage in themselves through riding horses. Their beautiful smiles as they galloped along with the horse to reach their activity goal always brightened my day. Contributions to society like this are an amazing way to impact your local community with so many serendipitous benefits beyond what you could have foreseen.

Ultimately, motivation is about turning your struggles into fuel to achieve what you want from your life rather than letting those struggles become roadblocks. Like anyone in this world, I've faced troubling times and moments of doubt. I want to share these experiences with you to show you that even in profound setbacks we can discover the motivation we need to keep moving forward.

Sometimes, we don't realize the adversity we are facing and how it shapes us. I was badly bullied at school, but over time I subconsciously blocked this experience out of my mind. Yet inevitably, these memories surfaced. Dealing with these memories taught me that confronting difficult situations can give us the motivation to turn those challenges into positive outcomes. For instance, writing this chapter helped me to heal from this experience! I remember sitting in the kitchen on a barstool upstairs in my mum's two-story home, discussing these past events with my mum and having an epiphany of how much they had affected me. My mum mentioned how I was severely bruised after bullies attacked me in the playground at the first school I attended at around seven years of age. This, unfortunately, happened on several occasions before I moved to another school. It's hard for me to recollect what happened; I believe our subconscious mind protects us from these horrific events. But the experience led me to be a little reclusive as I grew up, being cautious, risk-averse with my choices and somewhat of a perfectionist. Confronting

42

these memories motivated me to work through these traumas with a life coach, shifting the limiting beliefs that held me back from releasing my true hero from within. This brings me to share an important point that having a mentor, coach, or teacher to help you on your journey is vitally important. These are the people who can keep you going when your motivation for change wavers.

The second life-changing event I experienced was when my parents divorced due to domestic violence when I was ten years old. When my parents were shouting and pushing each other, I would try to protect my younger brother by holding him close in the nearby living room so he couldn't hear what was happening. Eventually, the police were called in. It broke my heart and world in two. The divorce court proceedings over custody were no better because I felt like a possession rather than a child in the middle of the family splitting apart. I felt confused, lost, and sad. It led to deep rejection trauma where I believed there was a lack of love, feeling quite lonely in those moments. As a result, I escaped into fictional worlds to avoid the painful reality of my parent's divorce. The coaching I have received to heal this area of my life is priceless. I learned to understand I am a miracle and this knowing motivated me to share my traumatic story with others. This is powerful because it didn't only heal mine but also other's wounds.

In hindsight, these two traumatic events helped mold the person I am today. Another moment of self-discovery happened at the age of 13. Being a night owl, I would often stay up late and one night, I came across an infomercial by Tony Robbins sharing how you could achieve anything in life by following simple steps. So, I thought, why not? It's worth a try. I took out my card and purchased the $200 cassette pack *Personal Power II: The Driving Force!* which, to this day, I still have tucked away on my office shelf. From this moment onwards, I saw an opportunity to achieve more in my life. Yet, if the above events hadn't happened, I wouldn't have found my way towards this beautiful road of self-discovery a solid source of motivation for my life. I now always

43

say to look at the good in any situation because you may find something about yourself you never saw before. Remember that life happens *for* us and not *to* us. Use these traumatic events to fuel the fire of your motivation rather than dousing it with water to drown your sorrows. These mantras or beliefs helped me plant seeds in my mind to grow a life aligned with my highest values. Potential power is only powerful when applied.

My life began to take flight when I assimilated those four powerful words: "I believe in you." When I found that belief in myself, it opened up many doors of opportunity. I recognize and attribute my belief in myself to the many coaches, mentors, and teachers who have aided me along my hero journey. The importance of the people you associate with is vitally significant in forming who you are. I've been around family, friends, associates, or loved ones that can either give you a hand up or bring you down. Their perspectives can contribute to you feeling motivated to achieve your goal or pull you down into a depressive state. Make sure you manage and protect your energy effectively to maintain a high-level state and keep your motivation intact. However, it's important to note it's not realistic to keep a "high-level state" at all times. We will go through the spectrum of emotions like sadness, anger, stress, fear, disgust, surprise, happiness, joy, peace, and love. I'm not saying only focus on the positive ones. True heroes go through life in their flow with all emotions. That is what it's like to live a full life.

This segues into my next lesson to feel the FEAR (False Evidence Appearing Real) as you go through life while acting in each moment that comes at you. FEAR can either hold you back or propel you forward. It's your choice. I never thought I had a choice in many down moments because I felt stuck in the mud, unable to move. I've experienced deep depression, anxiety and feeling disconnected from the world around me, including those closest. When I felt pain or was fearful, I would isolate myself and use my addictive impulsiveness as an escape from reality. My addictive nature led me to immersive fantasy worlds like *Lord of the Rings* by JRR Tolkien, *The Wheel of Time* by Robert Jordan, or *Game of Thrones* by George RR Martin. I gamed away 140+ hours or more of my time at two-week intervals to finish *The Legend of Zelda: Breath of the Wild* on the Nintendo Switch or the *Final Fantasy VII* remake on Playstation 4 while neglecting basic self-care tasks like grooming. Gaming sucked the motivation right out of me creating a false reality that made me feel safe but it didn't lead me anywhere. On my self-development journey, I realized that I was attracted to these avatars because I wanted to be like the heroic protagonists of these stories – like Zelda in *Breath of the Wild* or Cloud in *Final Fantasy VII*, saving the world from the clutches of evildoers. Finally, I found that if I felt the FEAR in real life, if I acted despite the FEAR, then the illusive ice blocks of FEAR melted away to leave a hero in their place.

Many a time I have looked up at the stars in the sky and contemplated how it would feel to live a whole life and be the hero of my story. I love movies, and one day had an epiphany: "What if I live my life like a movie?" It's possible to act now and start your story and turn struggles into victories! Now, I know you may be skeptical and thinking, "Anthony, movies are not reality." Well, I want to challenge that belief. Ask yourself, "What if? What if I could make my dreams come true?" I love the two representations below (i. and ii.) of living a full life because life is never a straight A-to-B course. Life is full of twists and turns to reach the desired destination. However, saying that, keep this rooted belief in your mind, "Life is not about the destination; it's whom we become on the journey!" I encourage you to sit and write down who you want to become in one year, two years, or even five years. Then, write down in the present tense what you will feel, hear, and be when you reach your goal. This is a powerful exercise of visualization to allow your imagination to go into a realm of infinite possibilities! Use it to stoke your motivation. A great book called *The Magic of Thinking Big* by David J. Schwartz comes well recommended to assist with this exercise.

(i.) How to achieve **SUCCESS** in your life:

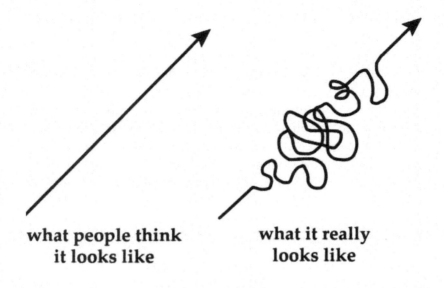

**what people think
it looks like**

**what it really
looks like**

(ii.) True representation of a **COLOURFUL** LIFE:

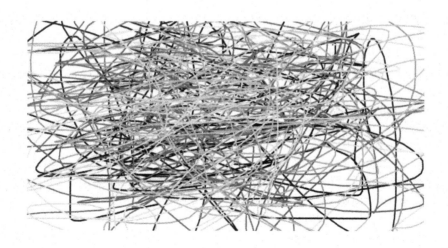

I believe everyone needs to find a spiritual connection since we deal with both the physical and spiritual realms when finding our passion and purpose. I will share my spiritual journey candidly to provide you with perspective on how I became a Christian and why it helped me discover my WHY fueling my motivation to live life out to the fullest. I started as a Catholic – not out of choice, mind you. My parents believed it would serve my younger brother and me well to be part of a religious congregation. We were christened as babies, and I also completed the Catholic rituals of confirmation and communion. I would often fall asleep at Sunday Church since, at seven, I didn't see the relevance of religion in my life.

It wasn't until my late twenties I reached a point of clarity in seeing the importance of my relationship with Jesus and our Heavenly Father. As an adult, to make sure I gave my life to Jesus, I chose to be baptized with two religious dominations. Unequivocally, in the short time I've been on Earth, I can tell you my Christian belief has helped me move in leaps and bounds beyond what I thought was possible. I will not say, with rose-colored glasses, that this has been easy. I have been tested and continue to grow in maturity towards Christ's identity. Faith can be an anchor that motivates us to strive for good works on Earth. To this end, though, through faith, belief, and action, I have lived a hero's life. I have the excellent fruit on the vine of prosperity, peace, joy, happiness, and most importantly, love.

One of my favorite scriptures in the Bible that speaks for itself, and I hold to as my highest value is, "Love your neighbor as yourself," from the book of Matthew, in chapter 22, verse 39. I believe God loves us all and living your life in God's love is something to be experienced personally, as an individual relationship with our Heavenly Father, because unconditional love will give you the motivation to take your life beyond what you thought was possible.

During my journey, I've learned life is so precious. One moment we are here on Earth from a physical perspective and the next, we are moving through the ethereal plane of the spiritual realm. As a Christian, every day I get up and take in that breath to live another day is a gift from our Creator, God Almighty. This hit home when I recently lost a friend to a horse-riding accident. When that terrible accident happened, this quote came to mind: "Life is a precious gift. Use your days wisely." So, with due haste, find that hero you've always meant to be. Take a leap of faith with one imperfect action – I can tell you from experience that a perfect moment will never exist. I've been chasing perfection for 30-plus years and found I was holding myself back because of FEAR of the unknown, trauma, judgment from others and my beliefs. The world needs you, your story and most importantly, your hero within. It all starts with the motivation for one imperfect action today, and then another, to ignite that fire within and show the world what you can do with your God-given gifts! So, I raise a glass to you for becoming unstoppable. God bless you.

"It's not what you've got, it's what you use, that makes a difference in how your life turns out."

~ Zig Ziglar

CHAPTER FOUR

———— ∞C✨⁀Ɔ∞ ————

Spiritual Motivation

By Marcia Quinton

From the start of my life, I have been awakened and spiritually motivated by unseen forces which are the living essence of the divine universal energies.

I have gone into the depth of my Spiritual Motivation and journey, to explain an aspect of my soul's experience with Spiritual Motivation. There are many millions of others, and we may not all agree on each other's truths. Yet we find ourselves with one connection: each has a spiritual foundation or has come from one.

"I have been inspired by spirit over the years and my passion for the truth is always near.

I have watched, with great joy, spirits work in developing other mediums. The light and hope they bring into this world is a great ray of compassion.

The amazing transformations of so many souls who have experienced this amazing awakening and growth and how they have shared their gifts with others to assist their growth and transformation.

From a small seed of light so much growth has opened doorways for many in life.

This is my goal to teach and inspire others to connect with the spiritual guidance touching their lives and open to it and allow that wonderful connection to grow.

This is a part of an everyday event, an everyday living experience.

Motivation is channeled to us all the time, working with spirit is opening to our connection the door between heaven and earth."

I was born in the country, with a remarkable ability to dream. I experienced many amazing visions that were unexplainable, and they continued to happen throughout my life, unaware that one day they would change my life forever. Throughout my youth, I had a profound spiritual connection happening within and felt the need to serve. One gift was my ability to know when someone needed help or support, and I never hesitated to give. This is who I am and the path my Spiritual Motivation took me.

So, this is my Reflection on Spiritual Motivation which has come from my experiences, growing up with many strange events occurring. Even at an early age I reached for the comfort of the church and through this connection, learned prayer, and to be still and peaceful, helping quiet things around me. So, my search for answers began early. This was the beginning of my spiritual motivation.

Spiritual motivation is a personal inner journey, an expression of freedom. It touches our personal and emotional feelings, lending us a willingness to explore and understand them and dive deep into their purpose in our lives.

Expressing our spirituality has not always been easy. Many protect that intimate connection for fear it might be abused or bruised. However, we are given choices when we are born by parental guidance and it's often for some a path they wouldn't choose, perhaps due to the nature of how it's projected by the religion or parents. We embrace it wholeheartedly when we are sure and confident about our spiritual foundation and can express it freely. It's a wonderful celebration. It's about acceptance of our belief that opens doors within and lets what is right for you emerge and grow unconditionally. Awakening your spiritual connections and freedoms enable you to share your experiences in every way without fear of being isolated or ridiculed.

I have found that Spiritual Motivation is a Powerful Mentor. It can take us back to the source that casts its influence within our lives and never lets us forget that, in our house, there is a Soul and its guiding loving force. A greater part of you that has yet to yield to the gentler you. In passing, we can all reconnect to our souls and see the condition of our souls that traveled through life with us. We all have the opportunity to restitute our souls. I am a great believer we can all change ourselves, our lives, and lifestyles, creating a better balance, perhaps repairing, and soothing the body emotionally, mentally, spiritually, and physically long before we pass over, enabling us to live a more fulfilling life.

Our greatest spiritual motivation is about bringing love, balance, and harmony into our lives. I have always believed that any spiritual link should be a gift of love and a continuance of that love toward others. It's a simple condition of the heart that helps us respond with that love to others. We love our family and friends and through this power, know that love is an endless source of light and energy from the heart. It propels us into giving service and care to others. Love lights up our lives; it's the most powerful energy we have, and we need to use and protect this beautiful gift.

I have always believed that I am an earth mother deeply rooted in life sharing the same pain and suffering of others to gain deeper enlightenment into the difficulties that they may face. I have always held steadfast as life is a journey and sometimes, we are not totally in control of where it will take us. My advice is to keep your hand on the wheel though to control your life.

Going back to the 1970s when I first found my way into Spiritualism, the teachings were not easily accepted as they are today. Especially in society, it was thought to be something to do with the devil and people took a wide berth of you, so you kept it quiet to continue with the teaching and foundation you felt was right for you. As I was working in the medical field, I found that what I believed was unacceptable in all ways, so again it would prevent you from sharing anything you felt or talking about your belief.

Practices and attitudes changed in some areas of the medical world when an amazing doctor took up the banner and educated us on the passage of death, dying and bereavement. Dr. Elizabeth Kübler Ross wrote a book *On Death and Dying* relating to death, life, and transition. It was through this deep insight I went to work in Palliative Care to assist and support dying cancer victims. She was a remarkable woman who eased the passage for many from life to the afterlife. To her credit, she was an incredible spiritual motivator to many individuals and still, her work is revered as it opened a door for many to consider also what is there after death. As a Spiritual Medium, I have found personal joy and inner spiritual motivation through this divine connection, and it propelled me to continue my journey through this belief and foundation. I had many defining moments through the years when my personal life was more at peace and had a stronger purpose through my relationship with Spiritualism, particularly with the people I worked with who were also connected and involved. The path that I chose was not always easy. As a student of life, a nurse, and through my spiritual progress, the motivation never slowed, only continued to flow strongly. I have witnessed many miracles in my time, with positive outcomes, where individuals sought the help of a medium and through their connection with spirit, left healed and in a better situation.

I recall a particular incident, when I was but a novice soul searching for evidence and truth, of going with a friend to see Doris Collins, a well-known English Medium and Healer. We attended her demonstration on stage and without a doubt watched as a man in a wheelchair rose and walk shakily across the stage. Another lady who was deaf heard again, and another with a tumor that just disappeared. All of these were verified by a medical doctor. I sat and was in complete awe that these acts happened and how dedicated she was and how motivated spiritually she had to be and what trust she had in those who guided her and reached out from the Spirit World to achieve this. The years of development and dedication to achieve in herself what a powerful compassionate motivation she had and all through her foundation and belief in Spirit.

Working with the spirit energies and intelligence is not just about giving messages to people. Spirit prepares us to serve firstly ourselves to heal whatever is within our lives that need attention, for there is no greater service than to serve the self. They have told me this prepares you to be clear and insightful of yourself before you assist others. This is important to the spirit guides, so we do not confuse our feelings, emotions, or issues and put them upon any client. There is a saying, "Know yourself and own what is yours and not someone else's and own it." Don't pass it on.

With time, spiritual awareness and growth awaken us to our most precious inner world, which is often discarded in the haste to survive and live in our physical world. We can achieve this through manifesting power and energy over time by seeking stillness and meditation and development to assist and enable us as a medium to become sufficient to bring enlightenment to life through us from them.

It's conscious energy that enables each of us to grow through our spiritual motivation and desires to serve and ensures we will be developed to handle the phenomena we work with. As we lean towards the paranormal, working with spirit is always shrouded in mystery. We differ from any other religion or service. Spirits motivate us through their service to help people and to contact humanity in providing a service and they will always strive to support us and help in any way that they can. For those seeking evidence from a loved one who has passed over, others looking for answers to what is happening to and around them, simply supporting us in providing comfort when needed. All mediums are individual and each one of us is called to serve life. As many mediums work in careers that already enable them to assist people in distress or need, this enlightenment helps them with their services and provides a protection element and healing with this energy from the spirit. Daily, I witness individuals who are involved working as a Light Worker. They are so spiritually motivated and dedicated to seeking healing and comfort for the many who need their services.

Each of us finds our spiritual motivation through our thoughts, from a calling within, through our heart's desire, and from our past and present teachings and beliefs. Our need to understand our spiritual roots is an ever-emerging situation today. To identify who we are, where we are from and how to sustain the hectic life we are living, to empower us to find a balance within all the chaotic situations around us. Understanding the self is perhaps the start of understanding others and their situations in life. It may only give us a glimpse, but we need to find a balance, and I believe that balance will come from seeking your spiritual self.

As I became more aware that becoming a lightworker was where my journey was going, I looked back at events as they happened throughout my childhood and early adult life. There were events out of my control and where no one around me understood me, so they put it down to me having a vivid imagination and dreaming. This was confusing to me, as these experiences were very real.

I experienced strange awakenings as if I was falling from a height back to earth. Afraid I would hit the ground this fear always woke me. And at other times I would wake with a terrible taste in my mouth and as if I was in a bubble about to burst; it felt like a capsule.

I used to get stories in my head about what happened to someone, and I knew they were not in my life; I always knew that they had died. I would know when things would happen by the feelings

I would get and feel sick about them sometimes. I was always seeking quiet places in nature. I would sit and dream and always drift off somewhere away from myself. I would always come back feeling amazing. As I became involved in Spiritualism, I realized this was all a part of spiritual awakening and this was gently motivating and preparing me for the path ahead. As a medium, my belief was founded on Spiritualism arising from there being no death as the soul continues into the afterlife.

My entry into Spiritualism came through a personal loss. I was a grieving parent who had lost my only child. I was at a loss, a profound loss. Accepting death as a reality. I understood but, in my heart, and mind, I was driven by some unknown force I could not accept. I would never see her again. It was a difficult time, and I was barely coping. I was working in a low-care area, and it was through this that I met a lady working with me. I was telling her about my daughter and the strange premonition I'd had two nights before she passed where I woke to a dreadful smell of death and a strong sense that my daughter was leaving. I watched her all night but with nothing happening, I put it down to a bad dream. The next night, the night she passed, she woke me and didn't need anything. She just wanted to play and be with me, and it was the only time she called me mum. By morning, she was gone. I never heard a thing during the night, not one thing. I have often wondered if her soul knew she was leaving and woke her to spend time with me so she could say goodbye. I have come to believe this to be true. The motivation was born to heal my pain.

My friend Irene then explained the afterlife to me, and that no one died. Their spirit journeyed to a special place called the Summerland (Spirit World). She had learned this through her mother involved in Spiritualism in England and was a great believer in this, and through personal experience. Her mum had fractured her ribs so instead of going to get medical help, she called a Spiritual healer who after two treatments of laying on his hands and asking for the spirit who worked through him to heal her, she had no pain, no bruising and was able to breathe comfortably and go on with life.

Spiritualists were unknown to me as I had never heard of them, so she explained some of it and then she encouraged me to seek a place here in Sydney to see if they could help me. The only place I could find was in the old yellow pages phone book, so I took myself off to the Enmore Spiritualist Church. Upon entering, I had this overwhelming sense of coming home, and it has never left me. I felt that connection growing with my daughter daily even though I questioned my mind and continued to search for undeniable proof.

I realized that we have a destined pathway to follow when we are born with few opportunities to alter that course or direction. Things will continue to reoccur until that goal is met. From my experiences and the many souls, I know that I have been the best to guide, support, and help. When I look back, I have seen the signposts in front of me for redirection and change. But as we often do if they are not clear and concise we fail to connect with them and miss the opportunities. We can all develop our psychic abilities, and if we build our Mediumship further, we can enable ourselves to communicate with the spirit world when we allow our spiritual motivation to guide us.

We can assist many in great need to connect with their loved ones who have passed over. This can be a form of healing when loved ones are left behind, helping them to seek comfort, knowing they are safe and ok. Through a medium's ability to communicate with the spirit world, they can bring communication and evidence of their continued existence and proof of survival. Information is usually personal and relates only to the individual seeking this form of communication. I have witnessed the relief on many a soul's face, knowing that their departed loved one is safe.

When people we love pass away, they are still and will always be an intimate part of us and our lives. The love we shared has not separated from us because they have passed, knowing the love we shared is still a strong connection and an unshakable bond that will link us for all eternity. In considering this, we believe that they look after us, it does not matter if we cannot see, hear them, or feel their presence. We in our hearts know that they are there motivated to support us from the other side. So many of us spend time talking with them in our head, out loud, when we visit their graves it's a ritual that deepens our connection with them.

My spiritual evolvement at the Enmore Church in 1973 is where I connected with my Spirit Guide Red Feather, a Red American Indian, who has been a Great Motivator throughout my life. He has guided my development and spiritual journey.

Red Feather has shown me his and spirit's great capacity to love unconditionally without judgement and to touch all who reach out in need. We need not be afraid to reach deep within, beyond the boundary's that life has set for us to spread this light to all and any who need it. This is a global infusion of love they are working with from the Spirit World and it's reaching out to many who have turned their lives around as they reached for more, a deeper understanding of self, life and through the awareness of others who have suffered and continue to suffer.

I have continued to follow my spiritual motivation and found a deep inner commitment to assist others and understand some of the experiences they went through, and their difficulty in expressing them to others as they were not understood, which created a need for them to look elsewhere.

So, in pursuit of answers, they found themselves drawn or guided to the Spiritual Church or medium where they felt comfortable. They felt welcomed and their stories and experiences were heard and understood, and they would also be given any help needed. As time passed, they gained insight and understanding of their experiences that separated them from others around them, who considered what they were experiencing was unorthodox.

As a teacher and Minister of the Spiritual Church, we provided Church Service regularly. Many people came and just sat, seeking to shelter within the church open to them. They asked no questions but were aware we were there to help if they sought it. I recall so many who came close to suicide, as they were in such despair over circumstances in their lives. It was a relief over time to see their lives turned around and they happily moved back to a balanced and happy life.

One such man, a friend I still have contact with today, came to the church when his life was a mess and was searching for a reason to go on. Love, in his words, had discarded him brutally, and he desperately needed help. As he was walking past the church, he felt motivated to come in. He spent a long time just sitting in the church seeking spiritual comfort and slowly he healed then sought his own spiritual motivation. He eventually went on to achieve a university degree, which enabled him to help and aid other men in the same situation he found himself in. He is one of the most beautiful spiritual souls you could meet in life with an open heart and the power to love unconditionally. He often tells me Red Feather was his initial guidance as he spoke through me on the first day, he came to the church. Through his healing process, he slowly found his peace and strength again and he leaned more towards his unfolding spiritual journey. He now lives by this unfolding daily in every way possible.

Through following my spiritual motivation and patience, I have been able to assist in the development and guidance of many mediums, healers, and psychics. To always seek truth, help people understand the afterlife and assist people going through bereavement.

My spiritual motivation have always been about healing and tending to those who need help, support, or comfort. We all suffer wounds, no matter what they are or how they were caused. You needed to be there for them as they reached out.

It's not a sacrifice to serve or assist if it comes from deep within with a desire to serve not only the spiritual self and the spiritual soul of another. Instead, it's a powerful responsibility to touch the vulnerability of another's life to hold that precious energy in your hands knowing they have complete trust in you.

All I have ever experienced with spirit, through myself and others, is love, caring kindness, and compassion, to help not to control.

This spiritual love, the unseen helping hands of spirit, has touched so many lives, some of whom may have been lost in the shadows of life. Spirit is freedom, an energy source, a living light, and love continually growing and surrounding us. As a Registered Nurse, I understood this. So when I embraced this spiritual journey as a gift, I accepted that I could relate completely to the wounds of humanity, as varied as they might have been.

So, motivated by Red Feather, I helped others, being there as a foundation to help their needs. To work for the Spirit World and help be the bridge for them between the two worlds. With my Spirit Guides, I have supported many of my students to move through life to assist others in need. Using their spiritual abilities, they have developed and worked with the guidance they were receiving from their spiritual connections.

Some of these souls have become gifted mediums privately and a few have become prominent public figures. Using their abilities how they have been spiritually motivated to do so.

Several of my students whom I have mentored, have produced Oracle Cards filled with spiritual messages and guidance. There are several more in progress. I have encouraged individuals to simply believe and trust in their connections in the spirit world and that they can achieve this and have.

I had great pleasure in motivating a class of my students to bring together the spiritual motivations they were receiving from their spirit guides and put them into an Inspirational Book which we called *Soul Pathways*. Then we had it self-published. I was guided and encouraged to do this, as it would prove to each soul the importance of the messages they were receiving from the Spirit World, and that these messages were not only for them but to share as a message for others. This little book may continue to touch others somewhere or spiritually motivate them in finding their path.

I have veered into other areas of spirituality and cultures, to broaden my spiritual journey and gain a deeper insight into what has been mapped out for others, not just myself. It creates a deeper understanding for me of what motivates others spiritually. It's not always religious or working within a spiritual connection. We are all on a spiritual path. Some of us are aware and embrace our truths. Others not so much. It helps us to understand each other's foundations, beliefs, and causes. It keeps our hearts and minds open, even if we cannot embrace them. After all, we all are a part of the integrated spiritual whole. I have learned that ignorance of other's feelings around their spiritual belief systems and foundations will disturb their spiritual balance and restrict mine. To stay open and embrace other's beliefs is a great spiritual concept we need to follow to integrate in a global sense. We weren't all born under one umbrella, but our one foundation is that we are all on a spiritual journey whatever the motivation is.

I have seen souls with an infinite connection that serves a purpose for them through their ability to serve humanity in some form, as it gives them a deeper inner spiritual calm by having been able to serve.

In the medical profession, I have witnessed miracles through the service and care of many of these medical professionals. Being a part of that opens the mind to each soul's power when awakened to its full intent. These are dedicated individuals willing to serve no matter how difficult a case or situation. This is the power of spiritual motivation at work.

They have such powerful abilities to transform the lives of others around them and seek no acknowledgement, but it serves their inner godliness. As you look at the thousands of services individuals provide through any care support system, you will see that the inner glow is there within each soul as they strive to help. They see conflict and sadness when all fails to secure that healing for an individual. They all suffer through these times, yet it becomes a strengthening and a more profound need to heal and help.

In my observation, I see that inner motivation as a deep desire, a relentless need, and a powerful compulsion to serve the soul and the spiritual nature of us all.

To awaken to this deep inner desire, some of us would be unprepared to express or accept that it's in our spiritual nature and spiritual DNA. More so, some would find it challenging to accept that we bring powerful energy through birth that will guide us on our journey. A soul's purpose, a possible life-changing experience we incurred through life, awakened the soul's desire and ambition, being touched through an unexplainable extrasensory awareness and understanding that powerfully motivated us. Some of us are

63

born simply knowing where our path will lead us, by being born into a family that follows a continual way to serve in some form through life. I believe this is possible due to continuing to be born or reborn for the same purpose of developing that soul group. For some, they just answer the call from God.

I saw deep, unrelenting compassion in a friend to go into some of the harshest situations in countries to help the plight of their people. However, spiritual motivation guided her to take this role.

This dear friend, who was once my student, had such a good soul and an unquestionable unconditional loving heart. They eventually became a teacher in the Spiritual Church for several years. She brought healing into many individuals' lives as a teacher and healer. Her touch is her power. Her words are her power. Her ability to see through the disturbed mind is a gift.

She answered the call as a Registered Nurse to help in East Timor during the invasion of the Indonesia army. This began a long journey for her where she spent the next ten years of her life, going to other countries working as an aid to support and help the people of Iraq, and Lebanon, and assisted in Tsunamis, supporting people medically and mentally to cope with the atrocities these communities experienced. In Iraq, she was helping to relocate displaced families from war and brought them back together where possible. All of this through her spiritual need to serve. She called it "service of the soul." Never once did she hold back at the risk of her safety and wellbeing, working with organizations that had security always in place.

Spirituality has always been there in some form throughout her life. As she matured it became stronger, and so did her desire to serve and help. We are often given life opportunities to expand our capabilities and prepare us for what may lie ahead. Her actions have spiritually inspired me, one being her bravery in putting herself in dangerous places to help others. Another is her drive to serve, and save others from conflict and suffering, a powerful spiritual motivator, which only strengthened my resolve to continue to support and help others reach their spiritual goals and keep them motivated.

Some of us will look back and see that our lives here on earth and our purpose were all about giving service to others in some form or capacity, and purely motivated through the spiritual calling we felt a need to heed, and inner unrest when we didn't.

Seeking Spiritual Enlightenment is an ancient ritual. Humanity has continued through the ages to gather to worship power, God, or Spiritual influence since the beginning of time. Our evolutional growth which has enabled us to refine and define our fundamental belief systems. Yet, the evolution of our Spiritual Motivation has remained unchanged. We are guided by the essence of this powerful energy and time has not changed it.

When the soul is inspired, it awakens the spiritual motivation, and if we are as humans able to rise to the call that has come through, then we can create miracles.

"We must have a theme, a goal, a purpose in our lives. If you don't know where you are aiming, you don't have a goal."

~ Mary Kay Ash

CHAPTER FIVE

―――――――◦◦◦◦◦◦――――――

Discovering Your Motivation with Knowing Your Purpose in Life

By Dario Cucci

A s a holistic sales coach, my clients always ask me, "How do you stay motivated during hard times?"

Some coaches promise that one can get motivated by simply applying specific exercises, and in all honesty, they do help, but they are only effective for a limited amount of time. They are, essentially, superficial.

I say this because, from my experience, there is an even deeper feeling that one has which motivates them to do things. It's a part of them. They just haven't found it yet.

What I'm talking about is being motivated not by action but by living your life with purpose, knowing how your actions will positively affect the world.

About four years ago, I was invited to be a keynote speaker at the M.E.N. Empowerment Network Event in April 2017 in London. And I got to say, I was so looking forward to being part of it because my dear friend Michelle Watson organized and hosted the event with her brother, Jermaine Smith. We were in constant contact to promote the event before the actual day to fill the room and sell tickets.

And I was told there would be at least 40 guests attending, so I prepared a PowerPoint presentation that would allow me to deliver significant value to the audience and sell my program at the end.

But things took an unexpected turn, because the night before, as I was tweaking my presentation, something happened that turned my life upside down in seconds. I couldn't believe that this happened for a second time and questioned at that moment what I should do.

There I was sitting in my rented bedroom studio in London, getting the final touches done for my PowerPoint presentation, which I was supposed to use the following morning when suddenly, I felt a painful cramp on the left side of my face.

After the cramp subsided, I suspected what it could be and prayed to God I was wrong. But I wasn't. I got up and went to the bathroom to look in the mirror. I only needed to look at my face for half a second before my suspicion was confirmed. I had another Bell's palsy attack.

For those of you who don't know what Bell's palsy is, it's when your face is partially paralyzed and cannot move because the nerves are damaged.

It can happen on either the left or right side of someone's face. But, unfortunately, it was on the left side and people who have it often think they had a stroke because the same thing can happen when someone has a stroke.

When I realized that I had a Bell's palsy attack, I asked myself, "Should I present tomorrow with only half of my face working properly?"

I mean, I had every reason not to do my presentation at the event because when you have something like this, you need to go to the hospital to get treatment and allow the inflammation of your nerves to settle down.

And because part of my face won't be moving, the audience might not even understand what I'm are talking about.

Plus, you don't exactly look attractive when it happens to you.

At that moment, though, I didn't care about it because my internal motivation kicked in, which gets me up every morning to do what I do as a sales coach, which is directly linked to my purpose to inspire and educate people with my story so they can have it easier in life. See, it wasn't the first time this happened. The first time I had Bell's palsy, I was living back in Australia, around several years ago, and there it took a different emotional toll. After I got diagnosed in an Australian hospital, I became depressed, lost, and didn't know how to handle it. I was also angry at the world and felt this was not fair. It took me about six months after the first Bell's palsy attack to get partial movement back in my face and once again find happiness in my life.

Even knowing what my purpose was as a result of the first Bell's palsy attack I had back in 2010, my emotions were all over the place. I felt I was being punished for having been loyal to the companies I worked for, putting my health last, whilst making their money a priority. However, one thing that occurred as I went through the emotional struggle, questioning my life choices, was that I realized, I have more clarity and drive than I had before. I didn't know why but I went with it. Today I understand it, but it took me a long time to get here along with a lot of self-work, seeing therapists, coaches, mentors, and friends who have helped me through those dark and challenging times.

But because I had clarity back in 2010 as to my purpose, it gave me additional motivation to work through all of it, to not give up, and to not let a doctor tell me there is nothing I could do except "take the medication, then wait and see if it gets better." I was not going to allow myself to be a victim, but I needed to find a way to become the hero of my story.

This kind of motivation is way deeper than the superficial one where someone tells you to "Get up in the morning and jump up and down for a minute or so, to feel the endorphins kick in to feel motivated to start your day." See after the second time I had a Bell's palsy attack, even when I felt frustrated that it happened again, not even a day before I needed to present, I had internal motivation and drive that overruled all the other limiting beliefs I used to have, such as "I'm not good enough" or "I can't be presenting in front of a crowd when I look like that," or "What if people make fun of me, because of the way I look now?"

Instead, my motivation was even stronger at that moment. I felt it was my purpose to find a way to present the next day. Instead of hiding it, suppressing the truth, or making excuses about my face, I would just be honest about it, so the guests that attend understand why my speech is a bit impaired. And if they could not understand what I was saying because of my Bell's palsy, they would tell me at that moment so that I could slow down my way of speaking as I deliver the presentation.

Since motivation is linked to your true purpose, you don't need external motivation when you know your true meaning. It's always within you and will drive you forward to get things done.

It's more challenging to discover, however, once you find it, it will never leave you, and become the hero of your life.

I first called my mum and spoke to her about it before going to the venue. I talked to Michelle about my situation, and she understood and offered me a way out. But I didn't take it.

In the morning, I started as the first speaker of the day and let me tell you, Bell's palsy was the least of my problems because a few things didn't go according to plan, one being that the confirmed audience didn't show up as expected.

Instead of 40 people, I ended up presenting to five. This can be demotivating, but I used it as an opportunity to show my adaptability. Instead of doing the prepared PowerPoint presentation, I ended up delivering a workshop-style presentation on the topic of "How you can optimize your communication to win new clients when networking." I asked one of the guests to join me on the stage so that we could do an exercise. I showed him ways to ask quality questions that build rapport with strangers who would be interested to get to know him. After the exercise with that guest, I spoke about reframing the interaction when they introduce themselves to a person they meet for the first time. Then the group did an exercise that showed them how to break it down into a practical script they can practice furthering their communication skills when they meet people at a networking event or a business function.

Those in the audience loved it, so I ended up winning a new customer who worked with me for over a year. And those that were at the event remembered the value they got from it, even six months after it was over. I know that because when I later met with Michelle, she told me that she still gets positive feedback from the presentation I did at the M.E.N. Empowerment Network.

The way I see it, there are three ways to have the motivation that helps us stay focused and on track with our goals.

1. The motivation of vanity is the external motivation primarily seen in the fitness, entertainment, and model industry. It's all about how one looks and is perceived. From the body to the face, we get motivated by looking pretty.

2. Through a mindset change, the internally created self-motivation, from things like self-affirmations, hypnosis, vision boards, s.m.a.r.t goals, and so on, concerns changing the mindset of one's perception, thus creating new positive habits that motivate oneself to keep moving forward.

3. The internal motivation connected to one's purpose in life is only then shown when one experiences a significant event, such as the first time I had "Bell's Palsy back in 2010. At the time, I lived in Melbourne, and the event caused me to question what I wanted from my life purpose, and it resulted in me moving back to Switzerland. This allows the subcon-

scious mind to unlock the hidden meaning of why one has been born into this world during the current time. Similar when one does self-development work consistently, working with a coach, attending workshops and seminars. It can also be that one has both had a significant event while also evolving through doing self-development work. Therefore, one need not exclude the other.

When I discovered my internal motivation through my life's purpose, it was a combination to keep evolving through self-development work—having an emotionally significant event that clarified my life's purpose, which is directly connected to my motivation, and why today I do what I do as a holistic business and sales coach.

The problem we have is that it's tough to stay motivated, especially if the motivation is superficial, skin-deep, and one has to pretend to be motivated to keep going because of all the issues one faces in everyday life.

Let's face it, in today's world we get distracted daily by ads, marketing, social media, radio, Spotify, Netflix, people, traffic, and the list goes on and on.

We neglect ourselves and the things we want to enjoy during our lifetime. Every year, during the New Year, we all set out with good intentions to change ourselves for the better, but two weeks later we are back in the same cycle of daily routine that stops us from actually doing the thing we set out to do.

One will argue it's self-motivation. The other will say it's the fact that they didn't have enough time for it. So what comes first, the motivation or having time for it?

The "MOTIVATION" comes first because if you have a motivation driven by knowing your purpose in life, you will make it work and make the time for it, as it then will become a priority for you.

As you read this, the next question you might ask is, "How will I know that my motivation is driven by my purpose and not superficial or just created by myself?"

You'll know when it happens because you will have absolute clarity and a feeling you never had before. It can stay with you long after it reveals itself. It will stay with you for life, and once you have it, it will not disappear.

However, once you do have it, you must follow it and make the changes in your life happen for the better. Because if you end up not doing so, you just wasted the "Gift" of being clear on your purpose that can motivate you to move forward and create the life you want to make.

Because motivation is, in reality, only a feeling that encourages us to give us energy that drives us forward in life and to make the most of it. One needs to step back and ask, "What actions can I take to achieve XYZ?"

"And what am I no longer willing to accept in my life, work, health, or business?"

It's important that once you know the motivation that comes from within you, which is connected to your life's purpose, you set clear boundaries and expectations, for what you want to achieve, and the actions required for you to get there and surround yourself with people that support you.

I, for instance, no longer accept negative people in my life. These people drain my energy, and are just there to take advantage of me, or put me down by projecting their limitations onto me or making their problems mine.

My mum calls them "energy vampires," and when I realize they are in my life I slowly but surely start to distance myself from them before eventually cutting them out for good.

See, the right people will not be jealous of your success in life. They will not try to use you to further their own life with little to nothing in return, and they will not be self-centered people that expect you to drop everything on a dime when they have a problem and need your help with it.

Instead, the right friends, family members, and others that come into your life, when they recognize your motivation and what you want to do with your life, will support you with love and accept you as you are.

They will also have their boundaries and expectations, just like you do, but they don't make their problems your problems, and they don't put you down or ridicule you when you tell them about your goals.

They might not always get it when you tell them what you want to do, but they are still there to support and encourage you whenever they can, without pressuring you to be someone you are not.

Here are three steps you can implement to discover what your life's purpose is, which then will activate your internal motivation.

The three steps to gaining clarity on your life's purpose:

1. Ask yourself, "If I had only one year until I die, what would I like to achieve for myself and why?"

2. Be in a quiet place where no one disturbs you, then close your eyes and ask your subconscious mind, "Have I lived my life with purpose?"

3. Then if your subconscious mind tells you "No," ask or even tell your subconscious mind, "What's my purpose in this lifetime?" Wait and see if it will be revealed. If it does not, relax more into it, ask again, and then tell the subconscious mind to "Please show me my purpose now."

It's important during this exercise you don't bring in your ego or critical mind that analyzes and tries to make sense of everything. Your subconscious mind does not work linearly. It's irrational and reveals to you your purpose unexpectedly. It might be that you get a vision, hear your inner voice talking to you, show you a particular word, or give you a feeling before it reveals a thought relating to your purpose.

Each person's experience is different. We all have various ways of processing our thoughts, emotions, and even how our subconscious mind works because the subconscious mind is directly connected to your soul. Each human has an individual soul, which occurs only one time.

So please don't get hung up on how someone else has experienced it and how you feel it should be or shouldn't be. Just do the exercise and allow yourself to go there.

If you feel you can't do it on your own, then you are welcome to contact me. My purpose is to inspire, educate, and train others to live a more fulfilling life. Including business owners to serve their customers at a higher level, to sustain it, grow it, and allow others to get amazing value from it.

See when you know your purpose, it will directly motivate you in every aspect of your life, which also means that if you are doing work for someone else or have a business that is doing well, but you are unhappy with it.

Then it will change the way you will go about it because when you realize that you are living a superficial life that has little to no purpose, that is functioning to survive or to feed your self-image, you will stop this as soon as your objective is revealed to you.

Seven areas in life will ultimately be affected by discovering your life's purpose and what motivates you to achieve your goals.

1. Spiritual
2. Physical
3. Intellectual
4. Career
5. Financial
6. Social
7. Family

When you change because your purpose and motivation are internally driving you, all these areas will shift your way of thinking, positively affecting your behavior.

It won't happen overnight, but over time you will adjust because of it, which is fine. It's also the reason I keep telling my clients why it's so important to have regular coaching sessions because as one evolves it's required of the person to stay accountable and have someone they can use as a sounding board.

I discovered my purpose over ten years ago, but from then to now I have changed. I not only have my own business now, but I also started living healthier, making healthier choices for myself, and have achieved a lot I set out to do. For example publishing my book, a business, spending more time with my family, or being featured in magazines and radio shows, such as Skynews.

Ten years ago, I didn't have my book, I was employed in Australia and unhappy. I felt stuck, my health wasn't that good, and I felt trapped.

All of that has changed so much today. Now I am living in Switzerland. I coach entrepreneurs, coaches, small business owners, agencies, personal trainers, and consultants to serve their customers better, increase retention, repeat sales, and win new customers without having to chase their tails or spend money on ads.

Since I now see them more often, my health has improved, I lost over 10kg of body fat, and I have a better relationship with my family.

Overall, I am living a more balanced lifestyle, because now I am creating the life I always wanted to have, a life that allows me to be who I am and know the importance of knowing my purpose. It's what gets me up in the morning and keeps me motivated every day and surround myself with the people that support my vision without having to compromise who I am.

Too often I used to do that, put my health on the back burner, to not even promote my business but someone else's. That has all changed today. Now I promote my business and make a positive impact with those I work with. I have strived to put my life's purpose first, which is to "Inspire, educate, and transform other people's lives for the better, so they can have it easier when they know their life's purpose, and as a result, will have the internal motivation to move forward."

"Today is your opportunity to build the tomorrow you want."

~ Ken Poirot

CHAPTER SIX

—⦿⦾⦿—

Motivated By Love

By Belen Lowery

In my small corner of the world, optimism and faith outweigh any negative thoughts that might rear their ugly head to ruin the day. Today, my daughter is about to be released from prison. With confidence, I believe Mariah has learned hard lessons and is motivated to make a good life for herself and her six-year-old daughter, Rosette. When Mariah was sentenced, Rosette was nearly two years old, and our family took over raising her until Mariah completed her time. It wasn't an easy adjustment for Rosette; she calls me "Mom" instead of "Grandma." But now, four years later, I am in Northern New Mexico waiting to pick Mariah up from the Women's Correctional Center. The time has finally come to take her back home, help Rosette adjust to being with her mother again, and help Mariah adapt to living free.

I'm not worried about the "small stuff"; it's the "big stuff" that I'm concerned about. Will she fall into the same trap as before? Will a good-looking young man charm her until she is under his spell and caught up in the drug and criminal lifestyle again? Will she be able to see when a young man is just fooling around and not serious about making a good life for himself? Forgiving herself for the past and moving forward to create a happy future is what she needs to do. But is she strong enough to resist the temptations a young single woman faces?

I look forward to the long drive back home to have a mother and daughter talk and give her advice. I have plenty of experience to draw on and made plenty of mistakes of my own. I understand that a young woman is motivated by love, that a woman's heart longs for a romantic partner, for someone she can love and who will love her sincerely and wholeheartedly.

Sitting in the lobby of the Correction Center, anxiously waiting for Mariah to walk up with her belongings, I keep Rosette entertained by talking to her and making her chuckle. Finally, Mariah walks up with a huge smile, full makeup on and her hair nicely done with a small braid on one side and the rest loose. Her long, thick black hair hangs down the middle of her back. She is a pretty sight to see! She says, "Hi, Rosette!"

Rosette stands up suddenly and says, "Momma!" They embrace for a while and just stare and smile at each other for a few seconds.

Mariah hugs me and says, "Hi, Mom! Thanks for picking me up!" I help her carry her bags to the car so she can walk while holding Rosette's hand.

"How's it feel to be free?" I ask.

Mariah says, "It's great! I never want to come back here again!"

"Just keep your mind focused on doing the right thing and you won't!" I tell her. "Plus, you have Rosette to raise!" I added. "I brought snacks to munch on until we get to Santa Fe. We can eat a good dinner once we get there. Rosette loves to eat just like you! You'll soon find out that she's so much like you!"

After getting buckled in, I play a CD with soft music as we headed down the highway. Mariah and Rosette talk back and forth and seem so happy just to be with each other again. They can't stop talking and laughing.

As we drive on, Rosette finally drifts off to sleep. I glance over at Mariah and ask, "What kind of music do you still like?"

She says, "Umm, I still listen to the same music when I was a teen, except I don't like to listen to the real bad stuff anymore."

"That's good!" I reply. "Music can be a big influence in your life. I know it was for me, especially growing up in the '60s and '70s. Mom would play country music during the day while she did household chores. That song by Ernest Tubb is still stuck in my head." I begin singing, *"Waltz across Texas with youuuu in my arms. I'll waltz across Texas with youuu!"*

Mariah smiles and says, "Oh gosh, Mom, I didn't listen to much country growing up."

"Well, I listened to all kinds of music! My sisters listened to pop, soul, and easy listening. My brothers listened to classic rock and Dad listened to Mexican music. Oh, the music would fill the air and I would just imagine couples falling in love! It felt like it was the generation of love. So many songs were about falling in love. Some were about losing love. I look back now and remember that my heart was full of passion. I longed for romance since I was a young girl. One time, Mom took my siblings grocery shopping, and I was left alone at the house. The song, Donna, by Ritchie Valens, came on and I turned it up full blast and start singing to it, except I changed the name to the boy I had a crush on—Johnny. I sang, *"Ohhh Johnny! Ohhh, Johnny!"*

Mariah and I both laugh, and she says, "Oh, Mom, you were something else."

"Did I ever tell you the rest of that story?" I asked her.

"Uhm, maybe! It's been a while if you did. What happened? You can tell it again! We have a long drive anyways."

The flat, dry countryside of New Mexico passes in a blur as we drive on. Rosette's still sleeping quietly in her seat. Continuing with the story, I say, "Well, to me, Johnny was good looking. He had blonde hair, blue eyes, and long eyelashes. He had a unique personality, but since he was one of the cutest boys in his class, I had a **huge crush** on him. I call it a crush because I was only in seventh grade when it started, and it continued until I was in eighth grade. I would write notes and put them in his locker. The lockers stood in the hallway in front of our classrooms; they had vents in the front, and I would stuff notes through them when I had something that I wanted him to know. Our family didn't have a phone, so this was the only way I could communicate with him. One time, my P.E. coach walked to the gym, reading one of the notes that I had written to Johnny. I was so embarrassed! I'm sure I wrote some crazy stuff there that I didn't want anyone to read, especially her."

Mariah laughs and says, "Oh no, I can just imagine what you wrote!"

"I was so lovesick! And you know that Mrs. Pearson was my favorite teacher and my volleyball and basketball coach too! I'm sure she got a kick out of it. She probably thought I was just a silly girl who fell in love easily. And honestly, she might've been right because when I liked someone, I **really** liked him. I opened up my heart completely. That's why I'm talking to you about this. I want you to learn from my mistakes and remember what I went through. Love is beautiful, but it can bring heartache if you're not careful. I was just twelve or thirteen years old and love—young love—was one of the only things in the world that motivated me. Let me finish the story because my heart still feels strange when I tell it."

Mariah leans back in her seat, her eyes tracking the road for a moment as the countryside slides by. "Sure, Mom!" she says.

"After a while, Johnny finally noticed me. We met a few times, sometimes alone and sometimes during basketball games. But, of course, we were so young; it didn't amount to much, mainly hugging. I don't remember that we kissed. I guess not! I would remember that!"

I turn to Mariah and smile. She says, "Well, what happened next?"

After taking a deep breath, I sadly explain, "Johnny wasn't that interested in me. He eventually liked some other cute girl. I was so distraught about our relationship ending so soon that I decided to commemorate it one night during a basketball game. I was standing in the girls' bathroom with some friends, and I took a lit cigarette, put it on my wrist, and counted for thirteen seconds."

Mariah says, **"Ouch! Why thirteen?"**

"That's how old I was. Maybe I was subconsciously marking this moment … my first heartbreak. **Look!** The scar is still there!" I lift my right arm to show her the little round scar right in the middle of my wrist.

"Wow, Mom, I never knew that about you!"

"Young and dumb, I guess. I remember Johnny every time I see the scar."

We drive on in silence for a little while, but something about the story is still bothering me. Telling the story has stirred up the memories again. "Did you know that I went to his high school graduation ceremony?" I say, breaking the silence.

Mariah asks, "Really! Why?"

"Well, my friend, Deedra, from Silver City, was dating Larry, who was like family. I grew up with him and his older brother, Pete, and Pete was in the same graduating class as Johnny. We ended up at their graduation party near the river. Everyone was standing or sitting around the fire, just talking. Johnny spotted me standing in front of the fire and he called out my name and started talking to me. He scooted over a little and tapped on the bench next to him so I could sit down. This was four years since I burned my wrist—in that time I had moved to Silver City and had a serious relationship with another boy. Johnny had a girl on the other side of the bench he was seeing, but he still asked me to sit next to him. He asked about my mother and the rest of the family. Then he told me about his plans to go to Las Cruces for college. Just small talk, but it was a nice conversation, especially after all the feelings I used to have for him.

"Not long after that party, Deedra and I head to Greeley, Colorado, to visit my brother and go sightseeing. A few days after we arrived, we were in my brother's apartment and Deedra was talking on the phone with her boyfriend. It sounded like they were just having a normal conversation, but when she put down the phone she turned to me—she looked horrified. 'You know what Larry just told me on the phone?' she said. 'Do you remember how Pete's high school class went to California for their Senior trip and went to the beach? There was a rip tide, an undercurrent... **someone drowned!**' I stared at Deedra and said, '**Oh nooo, not Johnny!**' Deedra widened her eyes in surprise, and I knew then I was right. I broke down and cried my heart out. Johnny was just eighteen and had his whole life ahead of him. It's still one of my saddest memories. Many people don't know that I have a scar because of him, though. Isn't it strange how things turned out?"

Mariah nods her head up and down in agreement. "How sad!"

"That love left me with a physical scar. Let me tell you about an emotional scar I thought I'd **never** get over!

"It's still hard for me to talk about my boyfriend from high school. We had such a good relationship for years and he even gave me a promise ring. We spoke of marriage and having kids and everything. He was nearly perfect, I thought. I always felt that he was better than me! Coming from a poor family, I felt inferior in many ways. I wore the same clothes over and over. Plus, Adam was the most popular guy in our class. He had looks and personality and he was a great athlete. Somehow we fell in love and were quite the couple! Oh gosh, that was so long ago, but it was some of my best times growing up. We had a great time as teenagers and knew how to have good, clean fun!

"Having a guy like Adam changed my direction in life. I was on the path of being a wild girl. He settled me down and we started on a spiritual journey together. We started reading the Bible and then his grandparents baptized me. I began my path in the Church of Christ Church. I had changed my religion from being a Catholic at sixteen. In those days, that was a huge thing. My family was definitely surprised! Soon, Adam and I went to church on Sundays and spent the afternoons with his family. His mother made the most delicious food and served it with tea. I remember feeling so blessed to be close to his family.

"During our Junior year, we had five classes together and spent many evenings together. I thought we were together too much, too serious, and too young! Our senior year was coming up and I felt we needed to spend more time with our friends, but I didn't think Adam would understand. I didn't know how to tell him, so it was a bad breakup. He said, 'I'm not leaving until you tell me you don't love me anymore!' I couldn't tell him that, so there was silence for a long time. Finally, I said it, just to break up the awkward silence and so he could leave. I watched him ride away on his ten-speed bike down the street, not knowing how that day would come back to haunt me. I regretted saying what I said for years. We stayed friends our senior year but never got our romance back. Adam became interested in a cheerleader and eventually married her. Believe me, even though I ended it, my heart was broken too! I didn't expect to lose him forever! That wasn't my intention. I just thought we needed a break from spending so much time together. But the truth is, I barely got closure from it these last ten years."

Mariah says, "Really, Mom? That long! Even though you married and moved to Ohio and led a different life?"

"Yes, even after all that," I reply. "I actually had a hard time in my marriage. John was so much older than me. I grew to love him as a companion, but I couldn't romantically love him. He was a good man and I respected him. I was a good wife, and he was a good husband. Our marriage worked. **But** ... there was one time, it lasted about a week when it was like I was being haunted by the life I'd missed. I was dreaming of Adam every night and it brought back the intense love I had for him and the heartache of losing him. Because I was a dedicated Christian, I would pray on my knees and ask God, "Oh Lord, please don't let me commit adultery!"

Mariah and I look at each other and we laugh. Mariah says, "Because of your dreams!"

"**Yes**! I felt that the devil was using the past to haunt my dreams! The dreams seemed so real and vivid! Here I was in a marriage that took committing adultery **seriously** and I couldn't go around with thoughts of another man in my mind while being married. **Our thoughts matter just as much as our actions!** This was very serious! Through prayer and staying connected to God and my Church family, I got through it."

"The devil always tries to ruin a good thing," Mariah says. "I can see how evil was always lurking in my relationships too! Things would start good and then before you know it, things would turn out crazy and bad. Just like what happened with Jerry and Daniel!"

"Yes!" I reply. "That's why I'm telling you my stories. You just never know what the future will hold. It's not going to be a straight path. It's gonna have **very** trying times and it's going to feel like you're being molded and shaped by **fire**. You need to stay close to God because you'll need Him to get through life. We're not promised an easy life, but we're promised that **He'll never leave us nor forsake us**!

"There are traps, as you know, that our enemy plans for us so we have to stay guarded. The Bible tells us to watch out for the *flatterer*! There are a lot of those ***slick fellows***! You're still young and beautiful and have a lot to learn."

Mariah replies, "Thanks, but I feel much older now. I've already gone through so much. The girls in prison talk about how scary it is to come out and start over. I'm not sure if I'm ready."

I grip the wheel. I tell her, "If you live by faith and not fear, you'll be fine. Just take one day at a time and trust that God will provide for your needs. He'll teach you, little by little. He taught me through the years how to trust in him. You're still as smart as you've always been. Plus, you have Rosette to look after, and she'll keep you busy. She's quite a character!"

We both chuckle and then Mariah says, "I know."

Continuing with my last thoughts, I say, "You see, I was motivated by love, romantic love. To find that special someone and spend a life together was the goal! My heart always had so much passion growing up and I didn't understand why. I was so eager to give my love away. I realize now that I should have been more careful. It was as though I was serving my heart on a platter, so willingly."

Mariah replies, "That's a bit dramatic, Mom! You were filled with a lot of love and needed to find the right person to share it with."

"Maybe," I say. "I had high expectations that were let down many times. Even after my husband passed, I wanted to find love again but found more heartaches and disappointments. Oh, how I tried! I tried until I was tired of trying. But I don't regret those experiences. I've learned to be happy without having a man to love. Yet my heart still bubbles with love and joy because I know that God is with me. If you'd asked what motivated me when I was young, I would have told you that it was love. And that's still true, only it's God's love that I seek now. Romantic love is lovely in its place and time, but romantic love is just *human* love! It can come and go and hurt you down to your core. I've come to understand that my relationship with God is **more important** than my relationship with **anyone else**. He's my source for everything I need, even love.

"You see, God made our hearts to carry love! You have to be very careful to choose the right friends and boyfriends to have in your life. Not everyone can love you the right way! It's up to you to choose who you will love and open up your heart to. Let God help motivate *all* your decisions. Keep Him close and whatever lessons you are supposed to learn in this life, He'll always be there for you through the ups and downs. His love won't fail you!"

"Thanks, Mom!" Mariah replies. "I appreciate you sharing your thoughts with me. I plan on being more careful with the friends I hang around with. Rosette and I have a lot of catching up to do, so she's my priority now. I'll remember what you've told me so that I'm more careful of whom I let in my life and in Rosette's life too!"

Nearing the Santa Fe exit, I'm satisfied that I've said enough and relieved that I shared from my heart. I take a deep breath and say a little prayer: Oh, Father, please guide my daughter in this new phase of her life. Help her to understand the difference between your love and human love. Share your love and wisdom with her and help her make a great life for herself and her daughter. I'm trusting in your love to care for her always and keep her from evil. Thank you! Thank you for your motivation and love!

"Knowing your purpose gives your life meaning, simplicity, focus and motivation. It also prepares you for eternity."

~ Rick Warren

CHAPTER SEVEN

An Evolution of Motivation

By Marie Chandler

As I approach fifty, I am grateful for the challenges I have had to overcome to survive. Now I am more peaceful and forgiving because this is my way to conquer fears, defeat my inner demons, embrace self-love, and remain open to the love and acceptance of others. However, it has not always been this way. I feel that overcoming adversity in my life has created the opportunity for me to reflect, reassess, rethink, and reframe.

I am the fifth of five children from a 'normal' Irish Catholic upbringing and was raised in the South of England. My childhood memories are of elder siblings being bigger, smarter, and stronger than me. They physically and mentally overpowered me in the games we played, leaving me with incredible feelings of overwhelm. My childhood inferiority complex led to a lifelong challenge of never feeling good enough. I had several tics as a child as my nervous system was discombobulated. My insecurity fed my motivation to work hard, ice the cake, put the cherry on top, and then add sprinkles – I never wanted anyone to ever accuse me of being slack. Over the years, I have realized that it's not what happens that matters, but how I respond to it to change the outcome. It's never about blame. It's about doing the work I need to heal and move forward. My life has and always will be about healing, growing, evolving, and living a full life.

From a very young age, I was motivated to try harder, do more, and fill the void I felt. If we had to read a page in primary school, I would read a chapter. If we had to read a chapter, I would read a book. If we had to read a book, then I would read two. Studying became my way of being. No matter how much I knew or learned, there was always more. The more I knew, the more I became aware of how little I knew. It seemed like I could never keep up and my efforts were never enough. This underlying unconscious driver is still present, and I must remain mindful to notice when I fall back into old habits. Never feeling good enough and not wanting to depend on others, I work hard to make enough money, put a roof over my head, and have spare cash to be ready to make the most of opportunities as they arise.

My motivation changed with age and environment, and life experiences have influenced me. Basic motivation, the 'carrot and stick' approach brought results and yet lacked personal satisfaction. As I learned the difference between conscious motivation and unconscious or subconscious drivers of my motivation, I understood the importance of self-compassion and celebrating achievements rather than simply moving on to the next goal. Life has brought me both expansive and contractive moments, and these situations have been the impetus for motivation from a survival standpoint. My life was greatly affected when I discovered Psychosomatic Therapy and the body-mind connection. It changed the way I viewed the world through different lenses. My journey became about personal rewards, self-recognition and fulfilling life through self-healing and helping others, and the different pathways that took me on.

I had always associated motivation with the 'carrot and stick' approach. I will elaborate on this for those new to this concept. To make a donkey move forward, you can jab it gently with a stick. Alternatively, you can hold out a carrot in front of the donkey, inviting the donkey to move forward towards the prize. Some people need to be reminded, harassed, or pushed before they act, while others require a target, a goal, or something to aspire to. I am that 'carrot person' when I have a clear vision and picture of where I want to go. Then I am happy to plan, create milestones, and tick off tasks. More recently, though, I have learned to evolve. When I have no clear path, I am learning to sit with the discomfort of stepping forward although not knowing where it will lead and allowing the way to reveal itself. Sometimes, the vision can be blurry, and if you don't follow a plan, there is no room for the possibility you could get better than you imagined. However, taking the first step reveals things you did not know at the beginning. So, while I have dreams, I am open to possibilities.

I am learning to understand that people are all different and we all have different motivational styles. Some people need the stick approach, while others require the carrot, something to look forward to or something that will drive them forward. I adopt the stick approach when there is an unconscious barrier in my way. Sometimes, I know what that is, and sometimes it takes a journey to uncover it.

We all have both conscious and unconscious motivations. Conscious motivation is when you are fully aware and have clarity regarding what you are doing and why you are doing it, and it completely aligns with your values, habits, and behaviors. Unconscious motivation is when you think you know exactly why you are doing something, however, there are often deeper reasons for your actions you are blind to. These reasons lie beneath the surface and influence your behaviors and actions. The hidden and unknown desires are the real reason for your actions.

I often wonder why some people overcome adversity while others metaphorically fall down the rabbit hole. Why do some people learn more effectively in calm situations while others learn better through the storms? I have noticed those in control of their emotions – people who respond rather than react – are the ones with better control over their behaviors. As time evolves, I am also bringing more of my unconscious into my conscious through play, face reading, meditation, and art therapy.

Psychosomatically, when you are learning something new, afraid, or things are not going your way, you make yourself smaller— this contraction serves as a protection mechanism. On the other hand, when you are confident and comfortable with what you are doing, you develop the ability to step up and take on more— this allows the expansion of your capabilities, and you will feel bigger and stronger.

Life has forced me into situations where I have had to dig deep to find the motivation to continue. This is where my self-healing journey has evolved, and it has taken me down many paths, some of which I wanted to take, and others where I have had no choice.

I have gained awareness of some of my motivations and drivers. I have a dose of "I'll show you," especially if someone undermines me or decides they know what is best for me. I am also motivated by the thrill and adventure of ongoing learning and continuous improvement. I welcome new experiences and opportunities to question things. When I was a small child, my mother used to say, "You don't let the grass grow under your feet."

Motivation helped me when I moved to Chamonix, France, at 19. My brothers had said I would never survive the ski season. Disappointed that they had no faith in me, I felt compelled to succeed, and I would not be going home with my tail between my legs. I funded the start of my trip with savings from a full-time job and three part-time pub jobs. In France, I made a living selling baguettes at night until I secured a position as a chalet maid, which allowed me to ski during the day and work at night. I also had several people who doubted my ability to sail from Sydney to Hobart across the Bass Strait in Australia, one of the world's most treacherous bodies of water. Some called it blind faith, but I had complete trust and confidence in my skipper. I trusted that we would not take unnecessary risks and would carefully review the weather reports and tide patterns. To sell her at the wooden boat festival, we had to get Saraband (the skippers beloved 10-meter Abeking & Rasmussen design Bermudian Sloop) to Hobart intact.

I spent much of my life unconsciously seeking recognition and external validation. The problem with this mindset is that when that external validation is not forthcoming, you feel like you have failed because you lack the wisdom of self-validation. I overcame this limiting mindset during my first Vipassana experience, a 10-day silent retreat where you are left to your thoughts. There is no speaking or eye contact with the other participants. You rise at 6 am and meditate. You adopt a seated position and are encouraged not to move for two hours. At 8 am, another two-hour meditation follows breakfast. At 11.30, lunch is served, followed by a long break where you can sleep, walk around the gardens, or lie in the sun. There is no talking to other people, no reading, no writing, no yoga, or any other form of exercise. There is more meditation in the afternoon, no dinner, and you finish with reflection in the evening and watching a video to understand the process. The experience is very difficult to put into words, but it profoundly changed my mindset. During the practice, I had mental and visual hallucinations. On the sixth day, I had a moment of elucidation that I needed no one else's approval. I replayed stories from my past, songs manifested in my head. Afterward, what I found most hilarious was the number of friends who were shocked that I stayed silent for ten days and completed the experience. A few thought I would bail out by day two or three. Interestingly, some people felt I could not sit in the silence of my own company and not speak to anyone – my friends did not know me at all.

Learning is a life theme for me and I'm open to the left of center ethereal experiences. My career in IT has provided me with opportunities to work across the globe in various industries. I have a strong passion for learning and a penchant for coaching and mentoring others. I worked as a software engineer for two years in the UK because I loved coding and problem solving before heading off on an around-the-world adventure lasting two and a half years. I returned to the UK for six months before heading overseas to Amsterdam, Netherlands, to join a small IT company.

I was motivated to learn a product and upskill my technical and functional knowledge, eventually focusing on APIs because I had that programming background. After a couple of years, I was inspired to move into management where I coached and developed the team. Then the opportunity arose to relocate to Australia and expand the Asia Pacific team hiring people in India and Japan while also leading a virtual global team with employees across the world. I took both technical and leadership courses and was one of the first people in a support role to be invited to Sales Club Excellence, enjoying a week in a luxury resort in Borneo, home of the oldest rainforest in the world and one of only two places where you can see orangutans in the wild.

After numerous travel experiences across the globe, I felt inspired to make fundamental changes in my life; my journey became about the journey within. I studied numerous modalities and collected nuggets of gold from each one, ignoring that which did not resonate with me. The NLP (Neuro-Linguistic Programming) certifications gifted me the clarity of my top three core values: ongoing learning and evolving new skillsets, efficiency and effective usage of my time and relentless independence. Those formative years between zero and seven have a lot to answer for. I see targets/goals as guidelines for what is expected of others. However, I need to set my visions higher and overachieve on my standards.

I always seek more efficient solutions to save time and be more productive. NLP has a modeling concept for identifying an exemplar's sensory embodied thoughts and actions and incorporating them into habitual everyday living. For example, I modeled a lady on her time management. She had daily tasks and weekly, monthly, and yearly goals. Each day she asked herself, "What are the things I don't have to do today?" Pure Gold! As jobs were moved to later in the week and month, she ticked off tasks, meaning she had the flexibility for other things. I loved this new concept which I embraced and embodied.

I learned that I have a long-running, deep-seeded pattern to always do things on my own. I had learned to rely on myself and not depend on anyone else (probably because they always let me down eventually). I also learned that my core values drive my behavior, and if I change them, I change my outcomes. I have choices, and I can change my mind. I can choose between surviving and thriving in the blink of an eye. I just need to ask myself, "What am I willing to do to achieve an outcome? What am I willing to accept? What am I willing to change and let go of?"

Challenging myself and questioning my values and beliefs became my top priority when I met Hermann Muller. Mueller is the creator of the Psychosomatic Therapy process who pioneered the art of reading faces and the magic of body-mind communication as an integrative process of self-discovery. He also co-founded the Psychosomatic Therapy College with Marie Mueller, and his legacy continues to this day.

I was a member of the Australian Board of Neuro-Linguistic Programming (ABNLP) and ran workshops in my home to create an environment for self-inquiry and personal growth. My NLP groups morphed into spiritual sharing, and then everything changed the day I discovered Face Reading and Psychosomatic Therapy. An introductory chance night watching Hermann Mueller share his story and I was up on stage volunteering my face for him to reveal to everyone Who I AM. I was amazed, intrigued, and inspired to learn more as he revealed my deepest fears, ingrained flaws, and embodied emotions. Someone I had never met before knew about my origin, my life challenges, and my gifts. Hermann could enunciate my habits, discern my attitudes, and link the embodied emotions, suppression, and repression, and swallowed words, childhood illness, injuries, accidents, and operations. I appreciated how my mind had been overruling my body for years. I could see that the body kept the score. He showed me where I was swimming against the tide rather than paddling in the flow.

The experience motivated me to signed up, complete the course, and I felt genuinely nurtured, and aligned at the end of the psychosomatic process. It was like a bed of roses, although it was primarily thorns that needed to be plucked. I remember having childhood flashbacks and moments of intense sobbing. The trigger point of emotional release therapy was comparable to ten rounds in the ring with Frank Bruno. On the final day, it was like a peaceful serenity bubble had been created inside me. I was finally out of my head and in my body, and it felt like a homecoming. I got goosebumps as I recognized the desire to teach his work to others. I felt a calling to learn how to connect profoundly and intimately, understand, have compassion, and embrace others for their different life experiences and let them know they are worthy. My tics had visibly reduced as the parasympathetic nervous system allowed my body to relax.

I had an epiphany as my face splits revealed that rules and systems ran my life. Irish catholic Mother, and a Father who did national service – there was a double set of rules to abide by growing up. I was not living freely. I was analyzing and planning, strategizing, and achieving, and I was not happy even if people from the outside thought I was. I spent an entire day documenting my psychosomatic history of significant life-changing events, accidents, incidents, operations, and emotional challenges. It helped me identify real pivotal moments in my life. When you see where your body has been affected, you learn to determine where you have embodied unfelt emotions. The only way to release those emotions is to feel them and then dissipate them. Easier said than done.

The impressions of others that influenced my behaviors and my need to learn and evolve took a toll on my mental health. My brain and demand for perfection, protection, and safety had become my prison. I could not embrace the day and live in the moment because of all the strict rules I had created for my life. While others had the freedom to do as they chose, I had stipulations, rules around spending, and plans for the future. I had forgotten how to

'Embrace the Now.' I had no idea where to begin, but I did know that I had to make significant life changes. Seeking freedom from my past patterns became my driver to evolve into another level of consciousness. It was time to get out of my head and into my heart.

This was a new level of motivation for me. I saw the benefits of setting goals and learned the importance of listening to my body. When the mind and body are aligned and on the same page, things appear to fall into place, living life is full of ease and grace, and there is a slowing down as we appreciate the small moments and learn to live fully in the now. However, it became apparent how life experiences made me contract when things went wrong. In those moments, I would disconnect, retract, and at the worst times, get stuck in my mind, frozen in fear as I was debilitated by analysis paralysis and at one with my ruminating mind. I have also had times where I have felt genuinely expansive. When things are going well, I feel safe and secure, supported, and inspired, and this gives me the impetus to try new experiences, which helps to expand my skills and amplifies my confidence.

I have often thought about the contracted periods of my life, the main one was when I ventured into the online dating world. I was gullible and, in hindsight, an easy target. I trusted too quickly and invested too soon with my heart and money. This was not some random prince from Nigeria or someone serving in the armed forces whom I could not meet. This was someone I met, so those dating scammer warnings were not on my radar. Until it was. I had become trapped with a professional fraudster. The moment I realized I had been duped, the ground disappeared from beneath my feet and swallowed me up. I was filled with despair, disbelief, and a sense of fear and insecurity.

Filled with shame and embarrassment, I took a week off work. I felt humiliated, which was exacerbated by the lack of concern and compassion in my interactions with the police. I joined online support groups and sought solace with other victims – this was not a rare occurrence. However, his abusive and threatening calls continued, and I was pushed mentally and emotionally to the edge. I doubted reality and trusted nobody. It took a few days of sobbing, reassessing, building a case on him, and revealing his different pseudonyms until I decided not to be a victim. At that moment, my goal in life was to protect other women. It became my sole purpose to remove him from society. After a long exhaustive campaign and my vertical learnings about the law (gathering evidence, providing statements, and eventually partnering with a reporter), I gained insight into police, detectives, local area commanders, process, due diligence, the court system, sentencing, victims of crime, and worked with the sheriff's office. Through that experience, I saw the legal system's flaws and challenges and how victims are not supported.

In the past few years, I have taken the journey inwards to a deep level of understanding and self-healing to recognize a story of resilience and how to reclaim my power. These learnings drove me to help others heal and see where they can support themselves and others around them. My love for learning and questioning everything sparked my motivation toward healing and making a difference for others.

Although the fraud situation left me emotionally drained, mentally exhausted, and physically debilitated, he did end up in jail. The psychosomatic response to minimize, an unconscious coping mechanism probably adopted from childhood, helped me survive the experience. The police and court process made me reclaim my power and balance out the wrongdoing. Within my greatest moment of powerlessness, I found a level of resilience I never knew I had. I also attracted an overseas client who had been in a similar predicament. I helped her gather and provide the evidence needed to serve an arrest warrant and assisted her in putting her perpetrator in jail. I learned that where there is a will, there is a way, and if it's important enough, you will move mountains to make it happen. I also realized that I still needed more skills.

Most people are familiar with the TV program *Lie To Me*, but only a few know that it's based on the scientific breakthroughs of Dr. Paul Ekman, psychologist, professor, and pioneer in the study of emotions and their relation to facial expressions, who interestingly did his research in Papua New Guinea, which is where Hermann Mueller honed his skills. So I studied his work, completing a course in Evaluating Truth and Credibility. I spent a week in Canberra, training with federal police and forensic investigators, where I learned more in-depth skills in face reading and micro muscle expressions.

My face reading and psychosomatic therapy practice attracted more people who needed healing. I knew that integrating the basic psychosomatic principles of focus, balance, and structure could improve their posture and breathing and help them manage their emotions. The face splits helped my clients identify where they were out of balance as they could see the visible differences between their masculine and feminine. They quickly see how their external world mirrors their internal experience. I am motivated by the changes and progress I see in them as they integrate those energies. Sometimes they are self-motivated, and other times sharing what I see in their face and body provides the impetus to make life-changing decisions. As I bring their unconscious barriers and obstacles into their conscious mind and use their body and history to show them where they have contracted in life, they discover their hidden power and motivation. We work together to break their imaginary shackles so they can progress. They learn that releasing their emotions allows them to move forward and that it's acceptable and sometimes necessary to retract.

As humans, we hold on to negative thoughts and emotions, which drag us down. Unlike humans, animals do a little body shake to release that pent-up emotion once the threat is gone. At that moment, they let go of their fears, appreciate that now they are safe, and move on. We can learn a lot from this behavior.

Sometimes, letting go of our fears, doing nothing, and taking the time out to heal is the best course of action.

I teach my clients that a mind is a powerful tool; constructive, favorable, and valuable when honed and focused. Attitudes reflect life circumstances, and when they reframe past experiences, this feeds motivation. I teach my clients to embrace the mind-body connection and be in alignment. When your mind and body are aligned, life flows and opportunities unfold, and it's easy to maintain your motivation.

Motivation for me now is about finding the flow of life, my center of balance, and inner peace. Too often, I have traded my needs to help others, leaving me empty. I have learned that I can only provide sustenance and support to others when my cup is overflowing. I embrace the desire to tune into the wisdom of my body and honor my journey, knowing when to adjust my sails for peak performance. I am excited about the new opportunities presented and grateful for being invited to be the enrichment speaker on cruises, and more recently, TV offers, *The Batchelor* AU, *Cheap Seats*, and a UK opportunity to face read the panel on *Loose Women*.

The most challenging period of my life was when I had to take a different path, and it was during those times I expanded my skill set and abilities, which I knew would benefit my clients eventually. It's always a humbling experience to be a beginner. Having a beginner's mindset ensures that you are gentle with yourself and aware of how much there is to know. I am motivated to be my best for my clients and to hold the space and show them WHO THEY REALLY ARE gently and compassionately. I work with people at the level they are at. There is no point in using corporate jargon and project management language for someone in need of love and light; equally, nothing is gained in beating about the bush when someone needs to hear it straight on the nose.

I have a passion for Astrology. As a Libran, I understand all too well finding the delicate balance and understanding the nuances of every individual. Someone may know fully they have certain contradictions in their behaviors, and others may become aware of the secondary gain for the first time. This means that although they have negative behavior, they get to experience something positive from the situation. Think of a woman or man in a domestic violence situation. They talk about the high highs and the low lows, and for some, the happiness and satisfaction derived from the high highs will put up with the consequences of the low lows.

For those clients genuinely ready to go on this journey; together, we will work on an entire psychosomatic history of your lives, looking at all of your relationships and situations from a mental, emotional, physical, and spiritual perspective, to provide you with some higher learnings and deep insights. We will also work on improving the posture as the body has messages of where we have embodied our emotional wounds. Healing can occur over an extended period or in an instant. I believe it depends on how attached you are to your beliefs, how willing you are to challenge everything, and how much effort or focus you are ready to put in.

I constantly question everything around me and seek opportunities to partner with the right people. Learning whom to trust and when to trust is part of the journey. Not all people who do bad things do so with awareness. We must all be mindful not to bleed over people because we have been wounded by someone else. Each day is a new opportunity to learn, an unknown reason to live and find what gives joy! The more I meditate and balance my nervous system, the calmer I feel. I have completed courses in stand-up comedy and comedy improvisation. Not taking life so seriously has also allowed me to relax more, and the tics have subsided. Following my newfound passion for volunteering, I have joined the Raise Foundation so I can be of guidance and support teenage girls, giving others an opportunity I wish I had been given.

My journey has taught me that admitting when I don't know, being vulnerable, and asking for help are signs of strength, not weakness. I have discovered that empowerment comes with trusting others. As I solve problems and resolve issues, I find a resilience that can only come from determination and humility. This positive attitude motivates me to stay solution-driven and help others as I share how you generate what you contemplate. I remind others that when they stay solution-driven and discover where they went wrong, they can correct their mistakes and possibly learn from them. Life is very rich and generous; it always offers new opportunities. You will always get another chance, another shot. This is what builds resilience and gives you the persistence and momentum to keep going.

So long as I am working towards being a better version of myself and bringing deeply unconscious habits into the light while improving and helping others, I am motivated and hopefully an inspiration to others.

"Your failures should motivate you to look at your life goals from a different angle."

~ Sunday Adelaja

CHAPTER EIGHT

Formation of the Success Mindset
How to Set and Reset your Success Mindset

By Hassan Magdy Saad

First period: 1988 – 2003
Hero to Zero

People tend to think that success depends entirely on being born into favorable conditions, but this is inaccurate. Yet believing in that concept of success leads many to their downfall. Winston Churchill once said that success is "going from failure to failure with an undiminished mindset." This goes hand-in-hand with a quote from one of the greatest minds of all time, Albert Einstein, who said, "Failure is success in progress." If we consider these quotes, we might understand that success is not always something you are born with. Although there are great examples of inherited success, this is not one of those stories.

To assume that success comes from thin air is a slippery slope toward failure. However, this story is not about failure. It's about intrinsic motivation in starting from scratch and working your way up. It's about a humble beginning that grew – and continues to grow – into something extraordinary. This chapter tells the success story of one person who developed the motivation to start from scratch and achieve goals that many people only dream of doing.

The subject of this story is Hassan Magdy, born in 1988 in the Kingdom of Saudi Arabia (KSA). Hassan was raised by a decent middle-class family with a luxurious gulf-region lifestyle. His father was an English instructor at one of the most prestigious schools in the KSA. In addition to his profession, he owned multiple local import and export businesses, which fueled the family's lavish lifestyle. One of the things that Hassan remembers of his family's extravagant lifestyle was the high-end German vehicles that his family owned. He enjoyed a life of luxury as he leaned on his father's wealth. But not unlike other fathers of that time, Mr. Magdy did not have plans for the future. He lived for the moment, driving the most expensive cars, setting his family up in the best neighborhood, and fulfilling his children's dreams to the fullest. Little did he know, the future would not be as kind...

The year is 1998. Hassan is driving a BMW, the same-year model. Like his father, he enjoys life to the limit without thinking of the future. He parties at elite clubs, eats at 5-star restaurants, and never thinks of tomorrow. However, by 2000, things got complicated for the young man. His father went through work difficulties, especially in his local businesses, where he began to lose money. He was forced to shut down the import and export operations and could no longer support his family in the style they had once enjoyed. Eventually, he had to send Hassan back to Egypt, where his life changed entirely.

When Hassan returned to Egypt, at first little changed. His father was still sending him pocket money, and he still lived a similar lifestyle to what he had enjoyed in KSA. He was still spending $300 a day, a sum of money that many Egyptians would earn during a whole month's work. He was largely unaware of the struggle that his father was going through. He continued to visit the most expensive restaurants, attend the biggest and most luxurious parties, and spend his time at the nightclubs that gave him the same feeling of the life he missed and longed for.

But after a year, the money well dried up. Soon enough, he realized that he could no longer enjoy the lifestyle he used to enjoy in the

KSA, and instead, was forced back into reality where his purpose was unknown and his calling unclear. Yet, one constant remained about him; the aura of success that had once hung on his father was perhaps the one thing that inspired him the most. Hassan's need to thrive was stronger than any other superficial need. The lavish and spoiled lifestyle he had once enjoyed needed to go away to force him to set priorities for the first time in his life. Even getting groceries had become a burden, which led him to sell the imported vehicle that his family had brought to Egypt during their first visit. Hassan knew that reclaiming the life he had once enjoyed would not be easy, so he did what he believed to be necessary to achieve success. His dependence on his father's assets had to go away, and he needed to rebuild himself from scratch.

While studying in 2002, he worked as a waiter, where he stayed for three years. The pay Hassan received was nothing compared to what he once had spent weekly, sometimes even daily. He adapted and thought carefully about his hard-earned money instead of spending it all right away. His growing interest in money management prompted him to join the Faculty of Commerce.

He realized that success would not chase after him, but it was he who had to seek it. Nothing would change on its own and time was against him. Yet, he remained optimistic, which was the first key to his success. He changed some of his habits to match his situation and instead of going to the most expensive and extravagant places, he chose more modest ones that he could easily afford from his work. He wore a smile despite the change in his lifestyle, which led him to the second step of his success. The situation he was in was nothing more than a challenge he needed to overcome to get back to the life he once lived. He was faithful he would overcome the difficulties and succeed.

Two choices loomed on the horizon: to dwell on the past or to believe and work towards a dream that seemed like a far-fetched and impossible point in the distance. Yet, like all inspiring stories,

Hassan chose to grind through and take the first initiative towards his goal, he was motivated by his fathers fall from grace.

Fall from Grace
2003 to 2010 – The Great Decline

The years between 2003 and 2010 Hassan recalls as the great decline. He encountered new, unforeseen circumstances. He was exposed to another side of life he was unfamiliar with. The uncharted territory would have filled anyone with despair, but even though he was not entirely comfortable with the changes, Hassan adapted.

His father finally returned to Egypt, having lost his fortune. Hassan was forced into the Egyptian schooling system, where he had to go through Secondary School, which was initially outlandish to him, but eventually, the young man adjusted to the system. Along with changes to his schooling, there were other changes Hassan had to meet. Instead of driving a BMW, he had to take the cheapest public transportation. This didn't throw him into a state of despair but motivated him. Whereas others would have succumbed to escapism, Hassan Magdy showed grit through constant success in his education. During the first and second years of secondary school, he struggled, but by the third, he was teaching younger students mathematics.

The most consistent thing about Hassan was his mindset; to believe in oneself, to think that one can climb back up after falling, is the willpower that many thrive on. Even though he was young and had lived a life that by many standards could be considered spoiled, Hassan had it in him to believe. That is the first aspect of the success mindset that everyone who strives to be great should have. But with willpower and hope alone, no one can overcome obstacles or reach great heights. Therefore, one should remember three factors even before developing a motivated mindset: belief, hard work, and a commitment to constant development and self-improvement!

Hassan had been gifted with a strong belief in himself, and his natural wit led him to one of the most valuable ways to pursue constant development: seeking knowledge.

Now, knowledge can vary greatly; one can learn things from a book or the street, but Hassan developed his knowledge through observing the successful people he met. He asked around about what could help him grow. He would ask successful people how they had achieved their goals and how to learn from failure. Although some answers contradicted each other, the young man filtered the accumulated knowledge and picked the constants of each story.

However, asking around and seeking advice was not the only thing Hassan did. To say he is a hard worker would be an understatement; Hassan spent his free time reading books, a habit he continues to have until this day. And while studying for Egyptian Secondary School was time-consuming, he chose not to waste time, but to invest it – an investment that would, later on, define the course of his life.

Instead of spending time with the boys, going to the cafes, or partying all night, Hassan focused on the essential things, which led him to be called a 'nerd' by his schoolmates. He was working while studying and in his spare time, but in both situations he was learning all the same.

By the time he completed secondary school, Hassan had asked what he should do. And from the knowledge and advice he had been given, it didn't matter which faculty he joined, what mattered was his level of success in whatever area he pursued. So, Hassan joined Management Information Systems (MIS) and quickly learned about the Information Technology Institute (ITI), where he questioned everyone whose advice he could get.

The successful people told him that the new department was good and that he should join it, so he did. While in college, Hassan's mind immediately moved toward work, which he couldn't do back when he was in secondary school. So, first, he worked as a waiter, and a captain order, before joining a newspaper where he quickly moved into covering the stock market, all while he was studying. The first business he started, however, was an Islamic Library. Yet his commitment to work didn't take away from his grades. On the contrary, he was more successful in his studies than most of his colleagues.

Once he started the Islamic Library, everyone told him he would never move on to anything else. This motivated, Hassan to overcome the challenges with this business. He didn't linger within the field. Instead, he continued to work and develop and became one of the top students in the new department in his college.

He had "too many balls in the air," but he managed to catch them all. Through that experience, Hassan not only became knowledgeable about the means of success, but also became very good at multitasking, and through the business that many people ridiculed him for – running an Islamic Library – he put into practice management skills that he was already reading and learning about. Though his goal was still distant, he could begin to see its shape, like the light at the end of the tunnel.

One thing that could be said about Hassan's experience is that he had created his mentors out of thin air. Whenever he would find a successful person, he would ask and let his curiosity flow; Hassan would seek knowledge and pay close attention to what he was hearing.

But Hassan also attributes mush of his intrinsic motivation to his faith in Allah. It wasn't just through the most successful people in business he knew he obtained his knowledge, but also through the more successful sheiks and imams. His readings were divided between religion, personal development, and management, along with the occasional books on philosophy.

His fall from grace was the spark that motivated him to aspire to greatness.

Final part: The Secret Ingredient for Success
2010 – 2022

"One of the things that kept me going is my determination; the routine I have brought into my life. When others slept, I worked on the next dream; when others slacked, I worked on the next goal," Hassan says with a smile on his face. His words are not a product of vanity, but pride in what he has achieved in his life.

The golden rule here is:

RTR (Run the Routine)

The third and final part of Hassan's story began at the end of 2010 when he graduated from college with a management information system bachelor's degree followed by a software development professional diploma from the ITI (Information Technology Institute). Hassan graduated as one of the most talented students in the programming field. However, that did not come by luck or chance. Hassan had spent his days and nights studying and accumulating more knowledge. He reaped what he sowed in becoming a top student by the time he graduated, a goal he had set for himself on the day he joined the new department.

He recalls 'motivation' being one of the most crucial keys to his success. Hassan claims that when he was studying, days became weeks and weeks became months, and by the end, he had stayed focused and achieved what he set out to while his colleagues slacked off and fell behind. Yet, motivation for the sake of motivation is meaningless; Hassan always had a larger goal in mind. He attributes much of his success to his beliefs and prayers, but he also knows that prayers without hard work would have done nothing. Motivation for hard work, discipline, and focus started his journey of success. Yet, that journey was only beginning when he graduated. It was not a journey without struggle or trauma, but before we dive into that, let us have a view of Hassan's daily life and how he separated the different aspects to cultivate a mindset for success.

Hassan says that he has five goals every day. The first is his religious one, which is praying on time every time; he always prays the Fajr prayer in the mosque at dawn. He reads the Quran daily to keep his spiritual mind cleansed and to confirm his connection with Allah.

The second goal he has is to live a healthy life. Hassan follows a diet and walks every day for at least 20 minutes. In addition, he goes swimming, plays football, and hits the gym every week.

As for his personal life, Hassan tries to finish at least four books per week. He also studies English to constantly improve his language and reads and develops his personal and managerial life.

The fourth goal lies within the family and his social life. Aside from spending time with his friends every week, Hassan frees up his weekends for family and family visits. He has three monthly visits to his family and reserves those days to keep a close connection with them.

On the professional side, Hassan's goals are far more complex. He set himself a goal of obtaining a Master's degree by 2018, which he achieved, and his dream then changed to attaining a PhD. He was set to achieve that goal by 2020, but due to the pandemic, he is still working on it. He works to double his salary once every three years and be the businessman he has aspired to be for so long. In addition to the books he reads, he sets the books in IT as a different task, finishing two by the end of each month. His motivation for success comes from witnessing the success of his father just as much as it comes from learning from his dad's failures.

These goals offer a blueprint as to how Hassan enhanced is mindset for success. By the time he graduated, he had applied and been accepted into a massive company in Alexandria, where he worked for months until he was fired. After six months, Hassan received one-months notice citing that his degree wasn't in engineering despite his degree being in ITI. It was not the nicest way to be released, as he still had a project he needed to finish by the end of his tenure, which he did before he was released.

Within a month, Hassan landed at Amazon, where he worked for a couple of years until he reached a point where his work was not challenging enough. He thought of business ideas and means to evolve, but he couldn't do that within the same company, so he found his way to another, where he landed a role as a senior programmer. Reaching that new height within his short career at that point, by 2013, was a significant step in his life. Where as most of his colleagues could expect to be promoted to senior-level positions after four or five years, he had done it in just a couple of years.

Hassan stayed with that company for nearly five years until once again he no longer felt challenged by the role and he decided it was time to move on. During his tenure, Hassan took only one day off per week, where as the rest of his colleagues took two. He would spend extra hours at work to finalize his tasks, evolve his knowledge, and study new techniques and methodologies.

In 2017, Hassan began working with CrossOver while he remained with X-Digital. He invested his money in projects in and outside Egypt. At some point, Hassan and X-Digital clashed, but he was quick to let go and while working with CrossOver and focusing on his businesses, he turned his sights towards TimeDoctor.

By the time he left X-Digital, Hassan had started a partnership with CrossOver and applied for TimeDoctor, where he was accepted. By 2020, Hassan had businesses in the KSA, UK, and Egypt while working with several companies.

By that time, Hassan had the golden answer to this question:

The Question:

Should we career-shift to blockchain? Or the stock market? Or trading? Or any other careers or industries to reach our first million?

We can use the first million to answer this question, as it represents an important step in financial success.

The Answer:

The millionth point is present in every field.

"This point is present in every field, but its age was not available to the majority. And if it remains open to the majority, and anyone can deliver it at that time, it will be a normal point. And it will stay at a more difficult point after which you can succeed."

Achieving your first million is a massive milestone in your success story and perhaps one of the greatest in material terms. Hassan claims that the same milestone exists within every field, but it takes discipline and willpower to achieve it. And while that milestone always exists, it's not available to everyone, making it unique.

It was a challenging goal to achieve, given Hassan's backstory and what his upbringing led him to in a round about way. However, his motivation, discipline and willingness to sacrifice the hours he could have spent sleeping, resting, or having fun have allowed him more time later on in life along with security and the joy of having achieved the success he had longed for.

Hassan claims that the Million Milestone exists for a special person, someone with the willpower that allows them to be disciplined despite whatever challenges lie in their background. Someone who insists on being more successful than the average. Someone patient enough to overcome any difficulties and stress. Someone whose level of intelligence is above average.

More important, the person who sets to achieve that milestone should be hopeful and not succumb to fear of failure. Once again, success is failure after failure but with the motivation persistence and patience to adapt and overcome. Risks must be taken, but with measured steps. If one fears taking a chance, one will never earn the reward that might come with it.

Know that it's not only through instrisic motivation, study, work, knowledge, or experience that one earns millions, but through every step one takes to reach that goal. Unfortunately, the path towards this success is not a red carpet but is marked by sweat and tears and lack of sleep, and even then there is no guarantee of success.

"Are you willing to pour your energy, passion, love, understanding, and intelligence into your field to become successful, or will you go with the flow and become one in the crowd?" Hassan answers when he is asked about the sacrifices to reach those dreams.

"Know thyself, first." He says that it is through your knowledge of your capabilities that you will achieve what you set out to achieve. So don't despair, don't back down, but insist on striving to be great. At the same time, don't be too stubborn to learn from your mistakes, don't falter behind, and don't fold under pressure. It's in **your** hands to be great and reach the success you have always dreamed of achieving.

"Remember, it's all about you. It isn't science, knowledge, or studies, but you and how disciplined and motivated you are. Those things will never earn you millions if you don't follow up and lead yourself on that path!"

"To unlock and unleash your full potential, you should make a habit of daily goal setting and achieving for the rest of your life."

~ Brian Tracy

CHAPTER NINE

Work in Progress

By Elizabeth Sim

Broken.
No one tells you how to fix the brokenness.
Your body quivers while emptiness swallows you as your tears go unnoticed.
Shattered pieces piercing from inside bleed till you hurt no more.

Run
You want to run back to him like always.
It felt right yesterday, so it should feel right today.
Run now before reality reminds you that you were wrong after all.

Cry
Tears are now normal, the gasping for air from crying.
You vaguely remember the last time normalcy meant smiling and laughing.
The cycle of happiness comes with tears because, to you, that's normal.

Every time I go through a major heartbreak, I would do something as drastic as cutting off my long locks, swear that I would never date another boy again, or write heart-wrenching poems such as the one above. Ok, I may not be a poet, and I know it, but I find that having a platform to express my deepest darkest hurt is a healthy outlet. Just ask my diary collection and many unpublished poems.

My name is Elizabeth. My friends call me Liz or Lisa. I am motivated by the never-ending goal to be my authentic self, live my best life, and piece myself together after completely shattering apart from heartache, disappointment, and failure.

The different motivations inspired this theme in my life. Let's begin with why I picked "falling apart."

I remember winding down after a productive day one time. I was about to let my hair down, sit comfortably on my queen-sized bed, turn on Netflix and binge the trending show of the week. I'd been doing well with my caffeine-free beverages and just couldn't seem to stop buying more choices from my favorite grocer. It was an Ayurvedic blend with echinacea, Rooibos and cardamom. And boy, did it smell like something out of a yoga retreat in India. It was an aromatic cup of contemplation. I looked closely at the box and this quote stood out to me: **"I am not interested where and what you have learned. I want to know what holds you inside when everything else is falling apart."**

What holds you inside when everything else is falling apart?

I was motivated not by the falling part of it all. I was inspired by the coming back or the reincarnation of a new me. Heck, I even have tattoos symbolizing the evolution of my growth. One was a bad decision derived from a chaotic and unforgettable girl's trip once upon a time ago in Calgary, Canada. We decided, sorry, I mean I decided to go with a sweet silhouette of a phoenix. I was asked, nay, blindly coerced to print my Phoenix right on a specific part of my body where "it'll hurt a little but will turn out sexy and awesome." It almost killed me and please never choose your ribs as your first location for any tattoo. It was a stupid idea! The second tattoo I obtained was when I was fiercely dumped on Christmas Eve many moons ago. I wanted to rid of this heart-wrenching string of unfortunate choices of men and discovered a symbol that stood for "New Beginnings." I loved it.

Nobody tells you how to start over when something falls apart, especially when it's your life. They just want to be there on the ride while you figure it out and take notes for themselves. But I slowly realized that the harder I fell, the more heartbreaking the incident, and I feared for my life because I had to adult harder. Which meant I had to ask myself, "Why?" "Why is this happening to me?" "Why can't I live happily?" So why couldn't we skip to the good parts? I guess life has a way of paving little gems of advice along your path to self-fulfillment and happiness. Stories about people falling apart and piecing themselves back together again inspire people. So, here's mine.

The Meaning Of Motivation

The definition of motivation for me shifted throughout my life. I once told a classroom of young people—when I was invited to give one of those inspiring talks about life and to go after your dreams and all— that there are two lives you could live: One I called the "Straight Line" life, or one known as a "Life Worth Living."

Straight-line life is where you're born, go to school, get a job, find the love of your life, get married, have babies, and have more babies. They have more babies; get old. Then bye-bye life. Hello, afterlife, that is if you believe in an afterlife. That's the straight-line life, from my point of view.

Where I come from, most of us were born and raised to do precisely that. I don't want to discriminate and say these expectations can be found only in Asia. That can't be further than the truth. So, when I contemplated my motivations in life, it had to come from the fact we were socially prepared from a young age to fulfill the straight-line life because any other life was unacceptable. Or just not Asian enough? I can only illustrate this coming from my experience.

The Straight-line Life

I was born in the hospital corridors on the 4th of October 1981 in a little town somewhere in Southeast Asia. I casually gave myself the nickname the tumor baby because the doctor discovered that I share my watery and slippery living quarters with an unwanted occupant – a tumor. Mum delivered me first before having her entire uterus removed because she was content with the offspring she'd birthed. Two boys and, finally, a decade later, a baby girl. Some say the best surprises happen when you least expect them. In hindsight, mum had no idea God had a different plan for her and blessed her with me. Oh boy. Was she in for a treat to how much misfit and mayhem I would cost her. Maybe I knew this from beyond the womb and that's why l was so excited to exist and popped out in the hospital corridors. Such an impatient baby!

Thus began the straight-line life journey with step one being born, check.

Step 2. Go To School

According to my mum, I was excited to attend school. When I was three, I would strut around the living room with all my school gear and be persistent about going to school the next day. But unfortunately, the school system at the time had a weird start date, and I had to wait till I was four before getting myself registered for kindergarten. So that meant waiting an entire year just so I could start school. What a bummer. My dad told me that when I did eventually start school, I would emulate whatever my teacher did through a regular performance. Dad said I would even punish him for not listening as my teacher punished us in class. You could say, that was a premonition to one of my hobbies or interests today. Not the punishing, the emulating. Just to be clear.

Frankly speaking, I don't remember a lot from my childhood. It feels as if I was one of those people who have had childhood amnesia. If I'd never asked mum about it or had I not encountered nor rummaged through old family photo albums, my childhood would never have existed. According to the most reliable form of online resources, Wikipedia. Childhood amnesia, also called infantile amnesia, is the inability of adults to retrieve memories of situations or events before the age of two to four years old and the period before the age of ten. This meant that my childhood memories were based on photographs and stories that mum and dad told.

I was sure I was a good student and daughter at least during my pre-pubescent years because I had no idea how to deal with emotions and boys. And as a child, mum was always the one who would tell you how to feel, how to respond and how to react to situations around you. You know, the "Look what aunty gave you, say thank you." Or "Don't say things like that, it's rude" or "Say sorry" because you made someone cry or used the word "idiot" as a response to people. Even if others have said it and a child should not. Mum and dad were pretty much the ones who designed circumstantial responses for me thinking that's how simple life was going to be. I realized soon enough that life, in this straight-line life, was more complicated than I could ever anticipate. That complication started with boys.

I felt like a latchkey kid growing up in my teen years because, by the time I was old enough to ask about boys, my older siblings were university students somewhere in the United Kingdom. My parents were mainly occupied with work or church stuff, and being in an Asian family, casual conversations about boys and all those juicy topics were deemed taboo. My dad's way of communicating his concerns and lessons of growing up as a teenage girl came in the form of books and presents. Once, he presented a bookmark which had "The Ten Commandments for Youth Today" written on them. Another time it was a piece of advice to keep the baby if I ever got accidentally pregnant. I mean it was sound advice for a Catholic daughter, but I wasn't sure that was what I needed to hear. But I mean, thanks, dad. A for effort.

Step 3. Socialization

Life couldn't be any lonelier. From the moment we were born, the amount of socializing we've been exposed to could outweigh the number of moments we were left alone. If you're anything like me, the house was always filled with people, toys, or animals. The people in my life consisted of my folks, my two older brothers, dogs, and housekeepers.

Being on your own was a nonexistent concept. Being the only girl in the family, you're supposed to have the easiest job. You get to look at your older siblings and your folks, emulate what's going on in their lives, and then make them your own. That would've been easy if your brothers were around often, and they let you tag along with them. Or if your folks spent more time with you instead of working hard. Not to sound like an ungrateful child, but there are gaps in a child's life that absolutely cannot be filled with toys, religion, or food. A child needs her family and when the family cannot fill that gap, they will turn to something else. Me, I turned to television shows, my dogs, and Disney movies.

Disney Movies & Divorces

In the 90s, living in Southeast Asia never exempted you from being a TV baby. You know, where your folks or siblings would introduce you to the best babysitter in the whole world - the Television. I mean its main purpose is to either distract you or keep you out of the way. So, most of my childhood memories mainly consisted of me, my TV and chicken wings. Apparently, Little Lisa loved her chicken wings growing up. There were many pictures as hard evidence. The best part is when Daddy came home with VHS videotapes of the latest Disney movies. *The Lion King* is the default answer should anyone ask me, "What's your favorite film?" I even gave myself the unique opportunity to watch it on Broadway, NYC, in 2018. It was like a dream come true for this little girl from Southeast Asia who loves her chicken wings.

No little girl could be deprived of the epitome of love, romance, and finding your knight in shining armor depicted in *Snow White*, *Sleeping Beauty*, and *The Little Mermaid*. I was addicted to my hunt for that Disney movie's happy ending. But, most important, I wondered if there was a handsome, debonair, and perfect male specimen that would treat me like a princess.

After being in countless failed relationships adding one failed marriage to that mix can shake that fantasy out of you. I have had my heart broken so often that I figured feeling emotionally numb, and empty was the way to be. The only way to appease the opposite sex was to mold myself into their ideal fantasy of a perfect woman. And so, there will be done.

Motivated by love I met *Andrew as a client when working for a bank. I was quickly attracted to his maturity and sense of self-reliance, and I shamelessly found an opportunity to contact him regarding a transaction-related matter. After a few business chats, the conversation turned casual. I happily tagged along to watch movies he liked, attend social events he had been invited to, and quietly observe how he lived his life. Andrew was about seven years older than me. He had "security" written all over him when I wasn't aware that I was seeking security then. After dating Andrew for a month, I found myself comfortable living in his tiny bachelor studio apartment, where he lived only a stone's throw away from his parents.

Our parents felt our living arrangement was disrespectful to our way of life, culture, and religion, so it seemed only fair for our families if we got married.

If you asked me than what I was made of I would have said family obligations, guilt, and an aim to please those around me. It felt like I was taking one for the team by relinquishing my right to say "no" because it made everyone else around me happy. I see many signs now as a divine intervention of sorts that told me not to go ahead with the idea and wedding. But my aim to please was much louder than self-respect. Maybe this was the Disney happy ending I deserved – being married to a man seven years my senior, who could provide me with the security my parents were proud to accept.

And so … we were married.

Within a few months of our marriage, I could already see the cracks that resulted in our eventual divorce a year later. Being a wife felt like a clouded journey. Wishing there was a manual or handbook to what I was supposed to do for this person called my husband, I did what I could and referred to my mother often for recipes because that was the only thing that made me happy - cooking. But food can only bring so much happiness to your relationship. Andrew was contented with the way we lived, but I felt nothing. I thought settling down would be the end goal for me. All the Disney princesses lived happily ever after, so there must be happiness to be found living a life of matrimony. So, I told myself to keep looking for it.

But failed to find it.

The Epiphany

> *"No one can make you feel inferior without your consent."*
> *-Eleanor Roosevelt-*

One morning, when I woke up and turned to look at Andrew as he slept on his side, I felt it. A rush of adrenaline that was, I believe to be driven by my pumping heart, my desire for freedom, and my longing for a happier me. I felt an awakening and decided that I had enough. I'm getting a divorce.

Being in a failed marriage wasn't the worst thing to befall me as a young Asian female. It was how the rest of society looked at me, stigmatized me and shunned me for breaking that sacred union. So being a 25-year-old Asian from a Catholic family living in a country where divorce was considered taboo back in 2006 was a whirlwind of a dilemma. There were moments of weakness where I would wear the victim hat and wonder, "Why me?" "Why do I have to go through this weary and pain-staking experience?" Yet on a good day, I garnered the unexplainable strength to practice obliviousness to the horrible rumors about me. I put on this veil of trust that somehow, something beyond and of a higher power protected me from pain.

I felt alone, broken, yet unafraid of what came next because something inside of me told me it would be alright.

And it did.

Lessons From My Divorce

All I ever wanted was someone to love me. When I think back to my past relationships with men, I realize how unfortunately naïve I was. The traits I grew up with in a Catholic household with devout parents were supposed to be something positive and something you were proud of. In everyone's mind, growing up with any religion means you grow up with values that would ready you for the secular world—the art of loving one another, helping the needy, the homeless and the hungry. Be kind and be ready to sacrifice your seat, your meal, and your allowances for someone else who may be even more tired, hungry, and need financial help. These were essential traits, but why do I feel dumb and stupid every time I get my heart broken? I questioned myself deeply and constantly asked myself if I wasn't giving enough, allowing enough, loving enough. "Did I not show him how willing I am to be his girlfriend?"

I never had anyone I could talk to in my family whenever I had boy problems. I had girlfriends who were always ready to listen and give their sisterly advice, but we were young teenagers trying to figure ourselves out. Still discovering what dating meant. I never needed to explore what I wanted; what my calling, passion, and purpose were in life in my younger years because all I was motivated by was marriage. You never knew what the fuss about self-discovery was until you had to live in someone else's world. Officially.

So to me, this had to change.

Fear Of Being On My Own

Sharing with my friends tonight about surviving high school and college I realized I was always in a relationship with someone. In high school, I was always hanging out with the popular girls, which meant shamelessly acquiring unnecessary attention from the boys. In college, I dated a guy who was super protective of me. I remember him teaching me about fashion and how to present myself. He even commented and taught me about caring for my oral hygiene.

This protective boyfriend made me call him from the school payphone every day when I was in Uni. I was a teenager with her daddy's credit card. When my dad discovered how much money I spent on calls, my boyfriend refused to pay his half of the bill. I paid my dad back with my allowances and was super disappointed in the guy, but I still forgave him.

Looking back at these experiences so far reminded me of how I barely spent time with myself in my thirties because I was so afraid of being alone. Maybe that's why I said yes to marriage than, it solved never being alone.

Despite all that's happened, I guess I am still hoping to have my Disney happy ever after because, I am still that little girl who loves Disney fairytale endings. I am looking forward to making that day the happiest day of my life. Why? Because I damn well deserve it.

A life Worth Living.

"What are you going to do with your one wild and precious life?"
-Linda Chandler-

"I am not interested in where and what you have learned. I want to know what holds you inside when everything else is falling apart."
-Anon-

What if I told you that sometimes the best life happens after you heal from a terrible decision? And I mean, an extremely life-changing one. When I felt lost and alone during my marriage, I lost everything. I lost my perspectives in life, I lost my motivation and most importantly, I lost my identity. The idea of being happy sailed away the moment I looked in the mirror and didn't recognize myself anymore. I wanted to cry but there were no more tears left in my body. What broke me was when my friends told me they didn't recognize me anymore. Not because I looked different, but because I no longer possessed the inner qualities that made me, me.

So, I blamed everyone around me for feeling the way I felt. For telling me that things would be ok. I blamed them for assuming I knew what was best for me. I blamed my friends and my family for not being there for me when I needed them the most. This affected everything in my life - my marriage, my relationship with my parents, the in-laws, my social life, and my career. I was so distracted by my terrible life I was also underperforming at work.

My manager called me into her office once and sat me down to her brutal honesty about me and my future in the organization. "Nobody wants you in their department, Liz, you've become a liability, and nobody wants you." I was applying for a transfer so hearing that kinda shook me. I realized I'd never heard a truth like that before. I liked it. In fact, I used it. Brutal honesty was probably what I craved this whole time. I felt motivated. I started exploring this feeling, this sense of freedom I felt when someone told me the truth. My Manager *Mandy also told me she would do her best to support me and help me get to where I wanted to go, but I had to wake up and pull my weight better. She said she would check in with me regularly on how I was doing. And she did. I eventually transferred to my preferred department, and it was there, that my life began.

The Beginning Of Change

My new boss *Lana introduced all the new joiners to attend this personal development program as part of our orientation to the job and it just so happened to be in Malaysia. It was the first time I'd ever flown out for any work-related event. Everything felt new and exciting I could feel a shift inside of me happening already. It was there I was introduced to so many powerful and happy people. There was dancing, sharing and lessons facilitated by many people with a voice, a mission, and a purpose to lead and make the world a better place. Starting with our hearts and our perspectives. All this was led by one amazing teacher named Linda Chandler. She sat us all down in this big room filled with eager students and just shared stories about a life worth living. I was blown away and worried simultaneously because I haven't been living this whole time. I was complying. Following the rules of a straight-line life, nobody said this wasn't the only way to exist. We simply lived that way because everyone else was doing it.

"What are you going to do with your one wild and precious life?" She asked. And that propelled me into a different direction of what life, my life could be. Linda had awaken my inner motivation, I started simply by saying yes to me, after saying yes to the divorce first. It activated a button I never knew existed inside of me. I wanted to live my life filled with my choices and my experiences. If I'm going to die my own death, I'm going to live my own life. So let the living, a life worth living, begin.

Say Yes!

"Surround yourself with the dreamers and the doers,
the believers and the thinkers. But most of all,
surround yourself with people who see
greatness within you, even when you
don't see it yourself."
-Steve Jobs-

I was lucky enough to have met amazing people throughout my change process and reinvention of self. I remember feeling inspired to refocus on myself, my dreams, and my goals. It wasn't about forgetting the pain I went through but redirecting all this mess and restlessness to better serve me and my soul's purpose.

Discovering my purpose lead to a new found spring of motivation and I started by joining this communication and leadership group at work. It was a collection of like-minded individuals that gathered together regularly and just spoke, presented, and had a great time learning about speaking. I was amazed at how the people around me seemed passionate and confident. That inspired me to look back at my old journals and diaries to revisit one of my favorite life goals – Being an MTV video journalist. I am a 90's kid and so in early 2000, it was a prerogative for every teenager to dream of being on TV (maybe it was just me, I don't know.) I wanted to uncover the secrets of the confidence these video jockeys owned as they spoke so effortlessly about music, celebrities, and other trendy stuff. Of course, I later discovered there were these visual aids and tech support called teleprompters that helped them, but you get my point. I was just enticed by that feeling of being in control of your confidence, your life choices and most importantly, your happiness. So, I started to see things differently. I felt warm and fuzzy inside, like a spark growing with each second of realizing how much I wanted to be happy again.

At this point, if you asked me what was holding me inside as I felt this awakening? All the fear, disappointment, and heartbreak drove me to feel dead inside at so many points in my life. It was as if, like a phoenix, all the bad memories burned to ashes and all I needed was a single reminder from someone else that I matter. My goals, my dreams and life matter. I need not be married to anyone to feel complete. I didn't need to subdue to a Disney-happy ending to feel happy. I felt new once more. Maybe helped by some higher calling, it was the only reason I felt so attracted to the Phoenix and why I have it as a tattoo.

The point is – I began my new journey in 2008 as an actual person after being asleep for so long. Finally, I was awake in 2008 and lived a life worth living. It took a circle of inspiring people, a group of passionate, like-minded friends and a failed marriage to teach me how to say yes to myself again.

I never became an MTV VJ. Although, with all the training and lessons I acquired from attending a self-development/leadership program called Core Values and a Communication and Leadership Training program called Toastmasters International, I focused on building a name for myself as an Actor and a Host in my tiny hometown. Investing in myself taught me to rediscover what courage meant and it started with my motivation of saying yes to one thing and then another. This snowballed into me participating in speech competitions on a local, then regional level. Which also meant I was experiencing more in my life rather than being a spectator of it. Within the next couple of years, I created new choices and checked off bucket lists I never thought possible.

Saying yes brought me to the World Championship for Performing Arts (WCOPA) in Los Angeles alongside talented artists. I challenged my acting skills on the world's stage in various genres, and we all brought home medals and awards, which elevated our love and passion for the arts even more.

I created my live talk show called Time Out With Liz, where I combined my love for food, music, and games—inspired by the likes of Jimmy Fallon and The Ellen Degeneres Show, while providing a platform for people to get up close and personal with local celebrities, personalities, and rising stars of the nation. The fantastic part of this experience was working with students or freelancers who were first-timers. So, networking with the youth and allowing everyone, including myself, to learn the ropes as we go along was precious and unforgettable. We experimented with online platforms, but they didn't make it. Hey, we weren't disappointed. It made us all realize how much we could achieve when we put our hearts and minds to it. (You can catch snippets of this little experiment on YouTube. Just type Time Out with Liz).

Despite going our separate ways, our paths still cross at different times and we are all doing the best we can to live our best life.

So no, I didn't make it to MTV. But I produced, directed, and discovered I could create content when needed. And that's pretty cool too.

I continue to say yes today, and I'm continuously surprised at the amount of untapped knowledge or know-how we have inside us, just waiting to burst through. All we needed to do was trust and allow ourselves to be free and just be ourselves on every occasion. You will be amazed at what you can do and contribute to in this life of ours.

Today I'm super proud of my accomplishments and can't wait to see what happens next.

What about relationships? How do I carry this spark in dealing with my romantic relationships?

Table for One!

> "Make peace with your broken pieces."
> -R.H.Sin

I haven't mastered this part and still make terrible choices. But I think I've accepted that I am a work in progress. I'm still making peace with all my broken pieces. I started going to therapy and I'm proud of myself. The idea of sharing your innermost thoughts and hurt with a certified stranger is not a popular nor a well-received concept yet in Asia. Just try asking your folks or friends to do it. Watch the reaction. But I know that in time, with a gradual shift in mindset coupled with people like me willingly admitting and validating there are people who can help. Then, maybe, we can normalize therapy to say, "Hey, it's ok if you're not ok." Because I know I'm not alone.

Today, I'm comfortable thinking that maybe a knight in shining armor may not exist. Maybe my friends were right about me not spending enough time on my own. So, I made it a personal mission to spend more time with myself. It can be super weird especially when you live in a place where table reservations are typically made for two at the very least. I remember the first time I called the local cinema to purchase a movie ticket for myself and the operator sounded slightly shocked when I wanted only one ticket. I was taken aback myself and sometimes back out of this one-ticket business. Or when you are on your own having breakfast while catching up on the latest Netflix series and someone says, "Kesian juga (what a pity), you're eating alone. Where's XXXX? (Insert the name of an ex.)

The more I thought about it, the more I realized it's a muscle that needed more flexing or reps. Being brave enough to reserve a table for one is a weak muscle. We just need to keep doing it until we are no longer afraid of eating independently. Because you're not eating on your own, you're just choosing "me time" over "we time." You are choosing yourself before everyone else. Who knew this simple decision could be a metaphor for something bigger? Some of you may already have that down successfully and that's great. Just remember that the next time you see someone else eating on their own, please be compassionate and empathetic that they may be motivated to live the "Life Worth Living" and it's their first time flexing that muscle. All of us are fighting our own battles. If a simple act of wanting a meal on our own is a step towards saying yes to themselves and living the "Life Worth Living," then celebrate that with them without judgment.

I'm Elizabeth Sim and I'm a work in progress.

"It always seems impossible until it's done."

~ Nelson Mandela

CHAPTER TEN

—⊸०≪⌒≫०⊶—

Rise: The Story of The Phoenix
By Kelly Wahl

We have all felt times of frustration. Frustration is an emotion that stems from a lack of control.

Many of us have sat in procrastination. Yes, sat. Procrastination is a place, a location, or a state of being. We set up camp in limbo between the past and the future, while not really being present.

Often that occurs after devastation. Devastation is what lies on the other side of a lack of control caused by frustration and the hurt of losing something or someone.

Yet even in the depths of devastation, eventually, we get a nudge, an *"awakening"* from some Universal Source or Higher Power. That is an inspiration! That inspiration opens up the doorway to motivation. Motivation is to put something in motion. So if you add inspiration, the calling to get out of your way, *to claim your worth* (no more limbo or procrastination), activate yourself and move forward; you will rise from the ashes of devastation and then the healing can take flight.

The phoenix has resonated with me since my youth. I've always felt like an underdog. Maybe it was middle child syndrome, but whatever it was, I always felt I needed to prove myself. Not so much for validation, but acknowledgment. That people would look up and notice what I'm capable of doing. Inevitably, I worked so hard for that acknowledgement that the pressure became overwhelming, and within moments of greatness, I'd crash and burn, sometimes from the fault of others but mostly from trying too hard. When I learned about the phoenix, this beautiful mythical creature that lives its life singing, soaring high, and then dies with its feathers fanning the flames to its demise.

I wondered, why would the phoenix ever spread its wings? Because of all it learned and experienced in that cycle. The phoenix then lays in its ashes, gathering itself only to rise stronger, more beautiful, and more brilliant than ever – its rebirth!

We all go through cycles, gathering knowledge and life experiences. Some are joyful, some painful, but they all make us who we are. It is then our choice to decide what we allow to define us. We can either wallow in the painful experiences and lay in the ashes with a woe-is-me mentality, or we can sit up, brush off the ashes, take back our power and rise victorious.

For my entire early years, I was unsure of what I wanted to be when I grew up. I had many jobs: I worked at a record store, sold men's shoes, and tended a bar. Eventually, I went back to school at a community college to see what motivated my interest. As an elective, I took ballroom dance. It was one of the few classes I enjoyed. I ended up taking any classes related to dance.

Despite not dancing early in life, nor having a "dancer's body," one of the main instructors saw my commitment, motivation and determination. As a result, he offered me the position of teaching assistant. I was ecstatic! He saw me grow not only as a dancer but as an instructor. He asked if I would be interested in taking up dance and theater as my majors. I didn't think that was an option considering I was in my mid-twenties – I thought I was too old. He told me about my "X factor" and all the possibilities that dance held. I could pursue theater, teach, and become a choreographer.

I was surprised when with his letter of recommendation, my passion, and my hard work, I was accepted into the university as a dance and theater major. I finally felt like I had found my life's purpose! I even had an opportunity with Disney! But, just as I rose like the great and beautiful phoenix and prepared to move to Florida, I got burned.

At twenty-six years old, I was diagnosed with cancer. I couldn't comprehend someone my age having cancer. Sure, I knew about young children with leukemia or older people with serious forms of cancer, but not me! I was in my prime! I had found my life's purpose!

Now, I look back and consider the diagnosis a "hiccup." I didn't have to undergo chemotherapy or radiation. Instead, I had medications and eventually an operation to remove all the cancerous cells, which were fortunately isolated. But at the time, the experience was devastating, demotivating and the depression I was plunged into was not fixed by an operation or by medication. Instead, I would wake up, eat a sleeve of chocolate chip cookies, take sleeping pills, and go back to bed.

I repeated this cycle for weeks. I had gone from dancing every single day, all day, being so active, to a drastic state of immobility. My body didn't know what was going on. My muscles were so tired and became weak. I then had to go to physical therapy five times a week for my body to relearn how to function and become stronger. I took a medical leave from school; I didn't go to Disney or dance again.

As I lay in my devastation, my ashes, I coasted through procrastination with no inspiration in sight. I couldn't face all the terrible questions – why wasn't I in Florida? Why don't I dance anymore? Why am i not motivated to do anything? My life moved in a different direction.

I was tending bar at a country club when I overheard colleagues talking about going to the US Virgin Islands and working for the resorts there. Since I was already set to move, I figured, why not?

Why not go to one of the most beautiful places in the world for the next six months?

You would think it would be paradise and maybe it is when you're a tourist. But, working there, I found many people in the same boat I was in. We were there to escape.

At first, it was fun. Waking up and drinking Mai Tais on the beach and not a care in the world other than lounging around until your shift started. But soon, the leisurely coasting through my day felt empty. I started exploring different beaches and different trails... Finally, I put down the Mai Tais and breathed.

I asked myself, "How can I feel sorry for myself when I'm sitting here on one of the most beautiful islands in the world?" It then dawned on me how some people will never get to see this view! They will never get to experience the peace of this island or swim in the clear blue ocean! I then realized that I was robbing myself of the gift of where I was: the present! I might never have made it to the beaches of St. John had I ended up in Florida. Maybe I would have been working so much I would never have had the luxury of time to travel. Or perhaps had I gone to Florida, they might not have discovered my cancer at such an early stage, and things might have turned out much worse! Sure enough, I could feel it arriving in the aftermath of devastation: inspiration!

I spent the next few weeks motivated waking up early, no longer cloudy-headed from self-loathing hangovers. Instead, I started each day not only waking up to the sun but rising with it! I was no longer playing victim to *what was taken from me*," but I looked out with wonder and awe, asking, "What's next"! That is what a victor does! The phoenix had been reborn with new life and purpose!

I wish I could tell you that everything after that was a breeze, that I was now walking the yellow brick road paved with opportunities, and that I was filled with vim, vigor, and motivation.

At times I would still get overwhelmed, and have moments of feeling lost, and my inner map would lead me back to the land of procrastination. When it did, I would recall that epiphany I had on St. John and I use that as a tool to arm myself when I feel uninspired and unmotivated.

As I learned the steps to this new dance, I was still plagued with the question, "What's next?" I thought back to the times when I felt most at peace, in harmony with my mind, body, and spirit. I remembered how massage therapy took me to a place where all three things were balanced. I had a particularly profound experience with one masseuse; I was so intrigued by how this woman possessed the ability to read my body, the stress, the tension, calm the chatter of my mind, and put a blanket of calmness over me through massage therapy. I thought, "That is it! That's what's next!" I wanted to provide people with everything I received in those sessions, to give them the healing I now carried with me.

Despite the skepticism around me, with people claiming that it was a fad and that I'd never be able to support myself or make a career, full of motivation I enrolled in a massage therapy program. Thirteen months later, I graduated and prepared to take my licensing exam. Once again, the phoenix had become more robust, beautiful, and powerful than before! There were eight weeks before the board exam, and I figured that it was the holidays. So I'd go out and celebrate. 'Tis the season and all.

I was out with work friends and had such an eerie feeling. I tried to explain it away; I was at a bar I wasn't familiar with, off the beaten path from my usual stomping grounds. But, as I was introduced to new faces, there was one in the crowd who the minute I saw, I didn't want to meet. My stomach flipped and the hair on the back of my neck stood on end. I told everyone I was calling it a night and said my goodbyes.

143

I went home, but even once I was there I felt unsettled. I heard a noise in the garage. I looked, and there he was: the man from the bar. I could see him through the glass panels in the door, cursing me for disrespecting him. He told me he would make me respect him and how he would do that. He broke the glass panel in the door and reached his hand through, trying to unlock it. I quickly put the chain lock on, pushed his hand away, and relocked it. We did this again and again. The next time his hand came through the window, I grabbed it and raked it over the shards of glass in the frame.

He backed off. I knew I only had seconds to figure out my next move. I looked for a knife, a cast-iron skillet, something! But there was nothing. I knew I had to leave the house and was out of time! I ran for the front door, unlocked it, and didn't look back. I kept running, hopped fences, and finally hid in some bushes. I didn't want to put anyone in harm's way.

It felt like I waited for what felt like an eternity before I heard a car. I heard two women get out, laughing and saying goodbye to the driver. I came out of the bushes, asked if they had a phone and explained that I had been attacked. The police and ambulance met me. In the hospital, I was told the cut down my left hand had severed tendons and nerves. My right hand was broken in two places – a "boxer's break" from defending myself. Until that night, I thought I had done everything right. I confronted my procrastination and unlocked the motivation that would propel me toward a better life. Yet here I was lying in the ashes.

I slept in the bed of devastation. Weeks later, the police followed up and referred to me as the *victim*. Hearing that word struck me to my core! I couldn't bring myself to utter it. If I called myself a victim, I felt like I was giving my attacker the power to take away who I am. Something woke inside me. I had come back from devastation before, and I could do it again. And this time, I knew what I had to do. I tapped into that spirit of motivation, that phoenix-like urge to be reborn. I was motivated by the incident to return to the all-women's gym I belonged to and did what I could.

Most of all, the gym gave me a safe place to gather strength. A group of crows is called a murderer, and a group of fish is a school; well, multiple phoenixes are called a choir! I was amongst my ensemble, and they were singing! They were singing I was strong. They were backing up that chorus in my heart: I Am Not A Victim, nor will I ever have anyone label me as such!

When the time came to take my licensing exam, I thought for sure I would fail it. The girl with her hand in a cast will be a massage therapist? One of my teachers contacted me and said that if you don't try, you've failed. If you try and fail, you will know how to do it better next time. What do you have to lose? Nothing. What do you have to gain? Perspective.

So I took that exam, breathing in deep breaths, inspiring my being, and oxygenating my brain. I took the test, and I was at peace. I knew that I had done all that I could, to the best of my ability. The rest was up to fate.

Weeks later, the casts came off my hands and I was no longer restrained. My right hand healed much like a golden glove boxing champion. My left hand had lost much sensation but was functional. I was whole again, mind, body, and spirit. I received my letter from the NYS Office of Professionals I was now a licensed massage therapist. So I not only had a job at an established spa, but I had a whole choir of clients waiting for their session on my table.

Months later, I spread my wings wider and opened my wellness center. After all my hard work, the Universe gifted me again! I fell into a gig working with Live Nation Concert Productions as the independent contractor for massage therapy. Not only was I privileged to be backstage with some of the top musicians in the world, but I also worked with the best "Boss" in American music history. I laughed and thought, "Disney, who?"

I wasn't just massaging those top billing act's stage personas; I was fine-tuning the instruments of entertainers who heal the masses through the gift of music. My story is one of the millions. It's not the beatdown that matters, it's the getting back up that defines you. Lying in the ashes is part of the cycle of the phoenix. It's the beauty of knowing that when something dies, it must be honored by rising again. It's in that act of advancing or moving forward that motivation is created. And that motivation builds up momentum and gives us flight.

Stay out of the land of procrastination with the power of being present. At times of feeling overwhelmed, release your fears with your voice. When you think that you are alone and lying in the ashes, know that you aren't the only person who has been burned. You are part of a choir. That choir is singing to you. They are singing, "Victor, victor!"

"Man plans and God laughs." So we must learn to laugh *with* Him and know He is not laughing at us. I invite you to take a page out of this book and use it to motivate your life.

"Act as if what you do makes a difference. It does."

~ William James

CHAPTER ELEVEN

---∽◦〜∽◦〜◦∽---

Motivation Through Adversity

By John Spender

It's often said that variety is the spice of life. I feel that adversity adds spice to life and variety adds sweetness. Undoubtedly, those who face adversity more often feel a stronger sense of accomplishment and satisfaction, which creates a dynamic personality. But how can we use adversity, without which we will never know true strength, as a motivational tool? I have noticed that all successful people are running away from their fears or running toward their goals. In the first category, we have the likes of Robert Downey Jr., who almost died from drug abuse and spent several years in prison. He had to hit rock bottom before he could rise again.

He used adversity as a springboard to motivate his life for a glorious comeback. Hollywood loves a real underdog story, and few can match Downey Jr.'s account of struggling for decades with drug addiction. He was in and out of rehab, consistently slipping up and landing in jail. He lost everything, his health, career, and family before he faced his addiction head-on and learn new empowering habits that finally led him to the *Iron Man* series.

Downey Jr.'s father introduced him to drugs early and he tried marijuana when he was only eight years old. Robert Downey Jr. struggled with substance abuse for most of his life. In a recent interview, Downey Jr. explained how doing drugs with his father became their way of bonding and this early drug exposure led him to spend most nights throughout his 20's and 30's getting drunk and stoned.

It wasn't until he began his romance with film producer Susan Levin while working on the film *Gothika* in 2003 that he committed to his recovery. They got married in 2005 and now have two children together. His commitment to recovering from addiction and reviving his acting career led him to his greatest success: starring as Tony Stark in Marvel Studio's *Iron Man* and *The Avengers* film franchise.

Robert Downey Jr. used rock bottom to rebuild his life and his family's stability to re-energize his life. So, what is your source of motivation when the chips are down? Sometimes life feels like it's against us and it's in these moments we have a choice. We can either slide further out of control into an earlier grave or find a source of motivation to bounce back bigger and better than before.

Downey Jr., now 54 years old, credits his relationship with his wife Susan, his children, Eastern martial arts, yoga, and the 12-Step program for enabling him to turn his life around. Addiction is a form of adversity; according to the National Institutes of Health in America, 10% of people will struggle with addiction in their lifetime. However, we all can overcome addiction and live a sober, fulfilling life in recovery.

Speaking from experience, in the late 90s, I had my rock bottom moment. Everything on the outside looked fantastic. I had a landscaping company with up to 15 staff on the tools. However, the pressure of the business took its toll, taking me on a downward spiral out of control. Weekly drug-fueled benders became the norm. I hung with the wrong crowd. I partied as much as I could. The full scene hooked me in; it was like being on a train that never stopped. When it did finally stop, it would be dramatic, and I would have a meltdown.

Because of my addictions, the quality of our work slipped, and I was spending my time trying to fix little mistakes but the mistakes became worse. Before I knew it, I had lost all my commercial contract work, or the contracts were drastically reduced. I struggled to pay for the penthouse apartment I had lived in for the last six months. At my lowest point, it was embarrassing asking my mum to stay with her and her partner for a few months, so I could stop the drugs and save money from the jobs I still had after all the clients I had been letting down.

Although I had lost my confidence, I stopped taking drugs. That stuff will put a big hole in your motivation for anything except getting high. It's a black hole that drags you down like quicksand. So, after five years of working for other people, I started another landscaping business that was more lifestyle-focused and offered international travel until I sold that business in 2010. After that, I began a coaching practice on and off for five years before moving into book publishing. I've been a book publisher since 2015, with over 300 author collaborations and counting.

When I started a new business, family and friends would tell me things like, "Now isn't the right season," and "It'll take you ten years to type your book the way you type." "That's a big transition to make," "Are you sure you want to sell your business?" Walt Disney was ridiculed for his animation idea, but he pursued his dreams until the world-famous Disney Studio became a reality. Walt Disney also went bankrupt pursuing his dreams in the early days of film production and almost lost his company a few times after the first bankruptcy. However, Disney never gave up and took on bigger films with massive budgets to push the limits of what was possible.

We have people like Albert Einstein and Steve Jobs who never gave up on their dreams. Einstein kept his wits about him, despite the constant ridicule he faced for his theory of relativity, which proved often to be accurate. Jobs was forced to make his first computer when engineers were skeptical of its success. He spent a lifetime trying to prove skeptics wrong and change their minds.

Anytime you try to do something out of the box or against the grain, you will experience pushback. However, never underestimate the power of your mind when focused on a definite purpose. If you see the lesson in every failure, the up in every down, and the reason for everything that happens, you will never fail to succeed.

Confronting your Fears

Every time we face our fears, we learn something new about ourselves. We realize that we're not made of glass that will shatter upon touching life's hardships. While I'm not saying we should be actively putting ourselves in dangerous situations, resilience is only honed by making ourselves vulnerable to our fears. We must choose how we respond by facing the challenge head-on when the going gets tough. The way I see it, the most powerful person on this planet overcomes their fears. Our fears paralyze us, compelling us to hide from the world, give up hope, and settle for mediocrity. But fear can be overcome. The question is, how do you get the motivation to confront your fears in times of adversity?

One way to push yourself out of your comfort zone is to use fear as a motivator. Being in a place you don't want to be can provide the extra motivation to move forward and achieve your goals. I wanted out of the black hole, to change my environment and the people I associated with and focus on rebuilding my self-esteem. It took a few months before I could move out of my mum's place and into my sister's old place. Two years later, I went on my first overseas trip with my then-girlfriend, and we had a ball.

The great thing about facing your fear is that it helps you understand yourself. It builds resilience and motivation charged with focus. When you're standing at rock bottom, you realize that there's only one way up; through hard work and determination. It takes courage of the highest magnitude to get back up after falling so far.

Facing our fears in times of adversity means we must get out of our comfort zone and absorb life's hardships. Being a slave to your fears makes for a depressing life because you're not growing. Fear is meant to guide; it's not a tyrant that rules your destiny. What are you afraid of? Are you allowing the noise of fear to paralyze your actions? The choice is yours. You can let the fear consume you or rise and overcome it.

Taking the Leap of Faith

When faced with adversity, we often question whether or not we should attempt what we have set our mind to achieve. We might examine the risks, chances of success, or even our sanity. In times like these, it's important to remember that if we give up, all our sacrifices in chasing our dreams will be for nothing. If we give up now, then our fears will have won.

Trusting our gut feeling is one way we can gain the extra motivation to make what seems impossible possible. It's what kept Walt Disney going when he was ridiculed for his fantasy of transforming the nightmare world of animation into an easier format to create films. If a grand idea doesn't leave you alone, then trust that it's something worth pursuing. Our motivation grows every time we move closer to realizing a dream.

That's what happened with the movie documentary I have been working on for the last six years. I started with a vision board with photos on it of all the thought leaders that inspired me along my journey of rebuilding my life after rock bottom. But unfortunately, I had no connection to them except by attending their talks or workshops. So, I would sit with my vision board in the mornings and evenings, talking to the pictures and having imaginary conversations.

One conversation felt so real, it was like having a telepathic discussion with Michael Beckwith about me flying from Bali to

Culver City in Los Angeles with a crew to film him. I did just that and everything came together like clockwork. It was like I was being pulled by a bigger vision than either of us. In February 2016, on a Sunday morning, I walked through the parking lot of Agape (Michael's spiritual center) with my director of photography and an assistant early. My DP was inspired by the pear blossoms and took a few still shots. Then, out of nowhere, a spiritual bodyguard shouts, demanding us to delete all the images.

He turned to ask why we didn't have media passes and what were we doing there. I calmly explained the vision for the film and our red-faced spiritual bodyguard said we had to meet Jaclyn Brown. We followed him to meet her, and I retold the idea for the film, and she looked at me with the most benevolent eyes and said "Well, dear, you have found a home here because that's the paradigm we subscribe to, welcome to our family." Everything was coming together so quickly I was blown away by the synchronicity of it all.

Then Jaclyn introduced me to Michael's assistant Leah Brown (apparently no relation), and she arranged VIP seating for us and organized the filming with Michael a few days later. All this started from an imaginary conversation that felt real enough for me to take a chance and believe in myself and the vision. Not long after Michael, I filmed Jack Canfield, Dr. John De Martini, Jessica Cox, and Lisa Garr. I had so much momentum and motivation that, with a little effort, everything flowed naturally. So I'm curious what moves and motivates you?

What inspired me about Steve Job's iPad innovation was when he trusted his intuition that people needed an iPhone with a bigger screen. At that time, tablets were unheard of, and devices were getting smaller. The iPad changed the game beyond recognition. And it all started with an idea and a leap of faith. Jobs was inspired by a dream that motivated him to bring it to life. His vision for a better future motivated his drive toward innovation.

We may question whether or not our dream can be achieved, but if you don't take a chance, you will never know. "Fortune favors the bold" isn't just some quote, it's a philosophy that has been proven in life often. Unfortunately, in times of adversity, it's easy to fall back into the old ways of thinking. All too often, our fears run the show and we give up on our dreams. This is the time to take the leap of faith and get off the couch.

Your dreams are worth fighting for, and your belief in them will push you one step closer to your dream. Life can be a struggle; you may have to fight fear, but it's far more important that you fight for your goals.

People who live their dreams are not afraid to be different. They stand out from the crowd and push boundaries to inspire others. That's what Thomas Edison did when, with little formal schooling, he became an apprentice to the country's best inventors. He grew tired of thinking small and set out to change the world of technology. His genius was rewarded with over 1,000 patents and the title "Wizard of Menlo Park." He was motivated by the joy of discovery and innovation. It fueled his curiosity to think of solutions.

In entrepreneurship, taking calculated risks is a big part of the game. But, of course, one of the most significant risks is to not take any risks; that's how we stay in our comfort zone and do the same old thing forever!

Know your Values

We all have our beliefs and values. Each person's values are shaped by the experiences we've faced in life and by who we are. In times of adversity, your values are what will keep you grounded and motivated. For example, let's say that you're great at visualizing the end goal: When you aim for something, you get a vivid picture of what success looks like. A clear vision of what you want to realize will be a tremendous support system in times of adversity. A clear vision adds fire to your motivation inspiring you to act. You will know that the result is worth struggling for because it's something you can envision.

Faith and hope are other values that will keep you motivated. These invisible spirits give you the motivation and strength to keep going when things get tough. Faith is to believe without seeing, while hope is to desire with the expectation of fulfillment. You must have faith in yourself and your goals. Faith will help you overcome challenges because it's an invisible force that acts like a life vest when everything else goes belly up.

Lack of self-pity is another value that will help you get through challenging times. Self-pity is not living. When you pity yourself, you're giving up on your dreams and letting your pain dictate how you live. Pity is the death of goals, but self-empowerment is the spring to action. If you feel sorry for yourself and hide your head in the sand, nothing good can come from it. By being empowered and motivated, you'll be able to make intelligent decisions about what steps to take next.

The key takeaway is that to overcome adversity, you'll need to tap into the values that will guide you and keep you grounded. Values such as faith, empowerment, self-motivation, and determination will allow you to rise from the ashes and pursue your dreams. In times of adversity, we often feel as if we're drowning. But, if you stay focused on your values and remain motivated by holding on to them, you will have more success than you imagined. That's the power of motivation, values, and the determination to achieve your goals no matter what obstacles get in your way.

Thomas Edison holds the record for having failed the most times before succeeding. If he gave up before perfecting the light bulb, would we be able to enjoy reading and writing in the dark?

Why should we embrace challenges when they come up? Because they strengthen us. They bring out the best in us. When we feel like giving up, adversity gives us that extra push to succeed because we know it will all be worth it. Are you going through a trial of fire? Know there's someone out there who has gone through something similar and survived! Look for advice from those who have overcome the obstacle you're facing right now.

Allow your motivation to guide you towards the next action step for your vision, dreams, and purpose. Move towards the impossible one step at a time. Have your motivation stretch and challenge the boundaries of your identity. I invite you to embark on your hero's journey and slay the dragons that guard your treasure.

"Out of the mountain of despair, a stone of hope."

~ Martin Luther King, Jr.

Author Biographies

Kaye Doran

CHAPTER ONE

Truth is beyond the shadow of the belief system. Kaye is a truth seeker with a deep desire to know, understand, reflect, and feel what is accurate. Then, she becomes a truth speaker. She is refreshingly down-to-earth, natural, and real. All journeys start with being inquisitive. As a storyteller, Kaye takes the complex and makes it simple, so you can understand, evolve, and grow. Kaye believes that life is our journey to integrate our physical and spiritual selves and to discover our truth.

Kaye is an entrepreneur, facilitator, writer, speaker, Women's Shamanic Leadership Life Coach, and creator of Inner Expressions; helping women realize their leadership from within. An unshakeable optimist, she lives with a foot in both worlds – physical and spiritual, working with her unique blend of gifts in connection, knowing, shamanic energy sound healing and accredited master life coaching. Kaye helps women who wish to create change in any area of their life who feel stuck, time poor, and overwhelm. She empowers women with self-worth and the ability to create change. Supporting them to feel and know their inner power moves them beyond their comfort zone and back into the driver's seat of their life. Kaye has been working with women for over three decades – and working on herself longer. Her motto is "the power of change is in your hands." www.kayedoran.com

Jamie Fair
CHAPTER TWO

With over 30 years of leadership experience and a dozen years in the interpersonal workspace, Jamie combines his passion for teaching leadership skills with his love of coaching life strategies.

Having been penniless and nearly homeless to achieving great heights professionally, financially and in his personal and spiritual life. Jamie uses his experiences to teach others to create motivation, push through fears, and overcome limiting beliefs to reach new heights in all facets of life.

He has helped hundreds in their careers and personal lives. From corporate teams to individual coaching, Jamie leads with a passion and purpose to help others discover what's possible.

Whether you're looking for your next career, an incredible relationship, or chasing your dream, he can help you see what's truly attainable.

Jamie is an SVP at a large tech firm, co-owns a $1M company and is launching his coaching practice. In his spare time, he is an avid scuba diver, traveler, hiker, reader, meditator, animal lover and gamer.

Jamie loves to hear from people who have used what he's shared to transform their lives. However big or small, if something from this chapter worked for you, he would love to hear about it!

jamie@fireuplife.com

Anthony Dierickx
CHAPTER THREE

Anthony Dierickx discovered the self-development industry after experiencing bullying and his parent's divorce at a young age.
He has been coached by some of the best coaches in this industry through their various materials, such as Anthony Robbins, Robert Kiyosaki, John Assaraf, and Dr John Demartini. Career-wise, Anthony completed his marketing degree at the University of South Australia in 2013 and graduated on August 19th, 2014.

He has travelled and explored different parts of the world from the Great Wall of China, the Eiffel Tower in Paris, the Islands of Fiji, Scuba Diving around Langkawi, Malaysia, Shark Cage Diving in Port Lincoln, South Australia, Kayaking with the migrating Humpback Whales in Byron Bay, New South Wales, Horse Riding in the Daintree Forest, Queensland, and more whilst spreading words of unconditional love, connection and community!

With his practical experience and Christian faith, he has guided others to live their optimum lifestyle. He has achieved this by coaching them to break free of their inner battles so they can learn to live in flow with their authentic selves and ultimately be aligned with their true purpose!

His mission statement – "To give a voice to the voiceless!"

He leaves a prayer of whoever reads this that God blesses you in every which way because this bio is not to impress upon you what achievements Anthony has done but to emphasise that if he can do it, you can do it! God bless you.

Email: anthony.dierickx@gmail.com

Facebook - facebook.com/anthony.dierickx

LinkedIn - linkedin.com/in/anthony-d-57773731

Marcia Quinton

CHAPTER FOUR

Marcia Quinton is a psychic medium from Sydney, Australia, born with enhanced intuition and the gift of premonitory dreaming. These gifts were latent within her until she sought guidance after the agonizing experience of losing her 8-month-old daughter to sudden infant death syndrome. The passing of her baby launched an intense seeking for spiritual connection and growth within her soul, which led her to serve humanity as a highly trained medium, teacher, and trance channeler of her guide, Red Feather.

Marcia was ordained as a minister in the Enmore Spiritualist Church, where she served for thirty-five years, giving countless readings, demonstrations, healings, and trance sessions. She also had a fifty-year career as a registered nurse. She spent the last five of those years with hospice patients, where she saw firsthand the work of Spirit in dying and was witness to many deathbed experiences involving patients and their loved ones.

In *Conversations with Catherine*, Marcia relays messages she has channeled from an entity known as Sister Catherine and insights she has gained through her many years of experiencing the transformative power of Spirit.

Contact:

61-0409-832-877

quintonm@bigpond.com

www.marcia.net.au

Dario Cucci

CHAPTER FIVE

Dario Cucci, is an International Speaker, Bestselling Author, and Holistic Business & Sales Coach to Professionals. He discovered that many Professionals, Experts & Coaches out their struggle to get repeat business, due to their lack of mindset, communication, and leadership skills & strategies in place, to support their growth.

His career in Sales started within the Self Development & Events industry over 20 Years ago, back in Australia when he worked with the Ton Robbins Team as a Sales Executive, based on commission-only income. During Daro's first year working with them, he generated over 1 Million additional Sales Revenue for the Company.

Seven years ago, he started his own Company "Entrepreneur Growth Ltd" which focuses on providing training, mentoring & coaching, with a unique approach to help them shift their mindset, improve their communication skills & strategies, and customer care structure. Dario especially loves small Business Owners and helping their employees, breakthrough their limitations, boost sales & build a stellar public reputation with their customer care service.

He wants to share his story with you, so you stop being superficial and work on yourself on a deeper level.

And if you are ready to not only sell your service but also figure out what your purpose in life is & how you can connect it to create your internal motivation, then reach out for a conversation with him by visiting www.dariocucci.net."

Belen Lowery
CHAPTER SIX

Belen Lowery is a Substitute Teacher at a local high school in New Mexico, where she enjoys the school environment and the opportunity to connect on a deeper level and perhaps, give sound advice to help students along their journey.

In true entrepreneurial fashion, she's always learning new skills, which are currently video editing and building a website called All Heart Woman.

It's Belen's goal to inspire and encourage women through her photography, poetry, writings and spiritual insights. She knows how life can be challenging and wants to be able to be a bridge for women to find true peace and lasting joy. Belen's dream is to travel, meet gracious people along the way and take pictures, of course.

Marie Chandler
CHAPTER SEVEN

Marie Chandler is an internationally recognised Psychosomatic Therapist, professional speaker, author, and coach. An inspirational speaker, Marie has presented at many key events and conferences covering topics such as 'The Magic of Hands and Feet,' 'Face Shapes Revealed' and 'How to spot a liar.' Her media appearance as The face reading expert on *The Batchelor* AU led to additional interviews on *Studio 10* and *Cheap Seats* in Australia and *Loose Women* in the UK. Marie navigates her face reading clients to rediscover their body-mind balance by shining a light on rejected parts to release suppressed and unexpressed embodied emotions. As her clients learn or remember how to self-nurture, this opens the gate for them to move forward with the alignment of their purpose.

Marie has travelled extensively, visited over 80 countries, and resides in Sydney, Australia. Learn more by visiting www.facereadingsydney.com.au.

Hassan Magdy Saad
CHAPTER EIGHT

Hassan Magdy, from Running Remote, has 12 years of experience as a remote worker and has co-founded three companies with workers in 10+ countries worldwide.

A strongly motivated Software Engineer, Web development enthusiast with a passion for system design and algorithms. With an exceptional eye for details and a sense of urgency when it comes down to problem-solving and always eager to indulge in new challenges, especially on the technical level.

Hassan has been a remote lead engineer on Staff.com (TimeDoctor. com) for a couple of years, Development head for ProCrew and LamasaTech, Teaching Web development for tons of students within multiple countries, and Academic Coach for over 32 technical publications (His most recent publication is 'Smart and Incremental Model to Build Clustered Trending Topics of Web Documents') and web development consultant for a couple of software companies, also he is a Ph.D. student now in NLP and Web-mining.

Find more about Hassan https://hmagdy.com/

Elizabeth Sim
CHAPTER NINE

Elizabeth Sim aka Liz is a Bruneian-based performing artist who received her formal education in Brunei, her B. A in Sociology and a minor in Communication Arts from The Kings University College in Edmonton, Canada, and a Diploma in Acting from the New York Film Academy (NYFA) in New York.

She's had an extraordinary and multifaceted career and creative journey as a Stage and Film Actor; a Talk Show Host; Columnist while working in HSBC Brunei for over a decade in Sales, Customer Service, Wealth Management and Human Resources.

Liz was retrenched in 2017 and that allowed her to dabble in baking and pursue her dream to obtain a formal education in acting from NYC. Today she is the Director of Human Capital Analyst and Development at a Business Consultancy firm; running her own online Gluten Free Bakery; A Co-Active Coach in training and an Acting Coach at a local theatre group. Liz is still actively performing on stage and acting in films. She's the youngest in her family of three siblings and the only girl. She lives with her parents, her three dogs, Lola, Trooper, Mia, and her cat Missy.

Contact Elizabeth for any collaboration by emailing her at elizabethsfsim@gmail.com
You can also visit her at:-
Instagram: @elizabethsfsim
LinkedIn: Elizabeth Sim

Kelly Wahl
CHAPTER TEN

Kelly Wahl is a *"Vessel for Spirit"*

Be it through body work as a massage therapist, energetically as a healer, consoling as an intuitive medium, or by her words as an inspirational speaker.

Kelly has been playing with Spirit since she was a little girl. She had many imaginary friends and would spend hours talking to the wind.

She later discovered those imaginary friends she had, weren't so imaginary after all; and *the wind* she was playing with was Spirit.

Kelly grew up in Buffalo, NY and loves being part of, *"The City Of Good Neighbors."*

Her family history includes her mother's great-great-grandmother, "busha," who was called a "see-er," connecting people with what awaits them.

On her father's side, her great aunts and uncle studied the scientific side of spiritualism: laws of attraction, palmistry, numerology, etc.

Encompassing both sides, Kelly blends her intuition with the founding principles of spiritualism and helps others realize that messages ARE all around us.

Whether it's a visit from a cardinal, *God's messenger*, finding *pennies from heaven*, or hearing a song that *connects* us to our passed loved ones.

Kelly wants to dedicate this chapter, and all of her work, to her father, Gary Jay, her hero, who has always encouraged her to not only dream - but Dream Big!

You can catch Kelly at various holistic fairs including New England's Natural Living Expo, serving in Lily Dale: the world's largest spiritualist community, and host of, "Connected with K Wahl."

KWahlhealingarts.org

John Spender

CHAPTER ELEVEN

John Spender is a 28-time International Best Selling co-author, who didn't learn how to read and write at a basic level until he was ten-years-old. He has since traveled to more than 60 countries, territories and started many businesses leading him to create the best-selling book series *A Journey Of Riches*. He is an Award Winning International Speaker and Movie Maker.

John worked as an international NLP trainer and coached thousands of people from various backgrounds through many challenges. From the borderline homeless to wealthy individuals, he has helped many people to connect with their truth to create a life on their terms.

John's search for answers to living a fulfilling life has taken him to work with Native American Indians in the Hills of San Diego, to the forests of Madagascar, swimming with humpback whales in Tonga, exploring the Okavango Delta of Botswana and climbing the Great Wall of China. He's traveled from Chile to Slovakia, Hungary to the Solomon Islands, the mountains of Italy and the streets of Mexico.

Everywhere his journey has taken him, John has discovered a hunger among people to find a new way to live, with a yearning for freedom of expression. His belief that everyone has a book in them was born.

He is now a writing coach, having worked with over 300 authors from 40 countries for the *A Journey of Riches* series http://ajourneyofriches.

com/ and his publishing house, Motion Media International, has published 29 non-fiction titles to date.

John also co-wrote and produced the movie documentary *Adversity* starring Jack Canfield, Rev. Micheal Bernard Beckwith, Dr. John Demartini and many more, coming soon in 2022. And you can bet there will be a best-selling book to follow!

AFTERWORD

I hope you enjoyed the collection of heartfelt stories, wisdom and vulnerability shared. Storytelling is the oldest form of communication, and I hope you feel inspired to take a step toward living a fulfilling life. Feel free to contact any of the authors in this book or the other books in this series.

The proceeds of this book will feed many of the rural Balinese families that are struggling.

Other books in the series are…

Awaken to Your Inner Truth: A Journey of Riches, Book Twenty Eight
https://www.amazon.com/dp/B09YLYMQ4H?geniuslink=true

The Power of Inspiration: A Journey of Riches, Book Twenty Seven
http://mybook.to/ThePowerofInspiration

Messages from The Heart: A Journey of Riches, Book Twenty Six
http://mybook.to/MessagesOfHeart

Abundant living: A Journey of Riches, Book Twenty Five
https://www.amazon.com/dp/B0963N6B2C

The Way of the Leader: A Journey of Riches, Book Twenty Four
https://www.amazon.com/dp/1925919285

The Attitude of Gratitude: A Journey of Riches, Book Twenty Three
https://www.amazon.com/dp/1925919269

Facing your Fears: A Journey of Riches, Book Twenty Two
https://www.amazon.com/dp/1925919218

Returning to Love: A Journey of Riches, Book Twenty One
https://www.amazon.com/dp/B08C54M2RB

Develop Inner Strength: *A Journey of Riches,* Book Twenty
https://www.amazon.com/dp/1925919153

Building your Dreams: A Journey of Riches, Book Nineteen
https://www.amazon.com/dp/B081KZCN5R

Liberate your Struggles: A Journey of Riches, Book Eighteen
https://www.amazon.com/dp/1925919099

In Search of Happiness: A Journey of Riches, Book Seventeen
https://www.amazon.com/dp/B07R8HMP3K

Tapping into Courage: A Journey of Riches, Book Sixteen
https://www.amazon.com/dp/B07NDCY1KY

The Power Healing: A Journey of Riches, Book Fifteen
https://www.amazon.com/dp/B07LGRJQ2S

The Way of the Entrepreneur: A Journey Of Riches, Book Fourteen
https://www.amazon.com/dp/B07KNHYR8V

Discovering Love and Gratitude: A Journey Of Riches, Book Thirteen
https://www.amazon.com/dp/B07H23Q6D1

Transformational Change: A Journey Of Riches, Book Twelve
https://www.amazon.com/dp/B07FYHMQRS

Finding Inspiration: A Journey Of Riches, Book Eleven
https://www.amazon.com/dp/B07F1LS1ZW

Building your Life from Rock Bottom: A Journey Of Riches, Book Ten
https://www.amazon.com/dp/B07CZK155Z

Transformation Calling: A Journey Of Riches, Book Nine
https://www.amazon.com/dp/B07BWQY9FB

Letting Go and Embracing the New: A Journey Of Riches, Book Eight
https://www.amazon.com/dp/B079ZKT2C2

Making Empowering Choices: A Journey Of Riches, Book Seven
https://www.amazon.com/Making-Empowering-Choices-Journey-Riches-ebook/dp/B078JXMK5V

The Benefit of Challenge: A Journey Of Riches, Book Six
https://www.amazon.com/dp/B0778S2VBD

Personal Changes: A Journey Of Riches, Book Five
https://www.amazon.com/dp/B075WCQM4N

Dealing with Changes in Life: A Journey Of Riches, Book Four
https://www.amazon.com/dp/B0716RDKK7

Making Changes: A Journey Of Riches, Book Three
https://www.amazon.com/dp/B01MYWNI5A

The Gift In Challenge: A Journey Of Riches, Book Two
https://www.amazon.com/dp/B01GBEML4G

From Darkness into the Light: A Journey Of Riches, Book One
https://www.amazon.com/dp/B018QMPHJW

Thank you to all the authors who have shared aspects of their lives, hoping to inspire others to live a bigger version of themselves.

I want to share a beautiful quote from the great Jim Rohan, "You can't complain and feel grateful at the same time." At any given moment, we have a choice to either feel like a victim of life or be connected and grateful for it. I hope this book helps you to feel grateful and inspires you to go after your dreams.

For more information about contributing to the series, visit http://ajourneyofriches.com/. Furthermore, if you enjoyed reading this book, we would appreciate your review on Amazon to help get our message out to even more readers.

Made in USA - North Chelmsford, MA
1338331_9781925919462
10.31.2022 1617